SOUTHERN MAKERS

SOUTHERN MAKERS

Food, **Design**, **Craft**, and Other Scenes from the Tactile Life

JENNIFER CAUSEY

Foreword by Grace Bonney

Princeton Architectural Press, New York

Contents

·❦◇❦·

·❦◇❦·

Foreword

·❧◇❧·

Grace Bonney, founder of Design*Sponge

There is something special about the South. Whether you were born there or just passed through, to spend time in the South is to love the South.

I was born in Virginia Beach—the least "Southern" part of Virginia. Growing up there was a bit like growing up in a city such as Austin or Portland. It was a strange outcropping that was unlike the majority of the state surrounding it. Thankfully my grandparents lived in the Shenandoah Valley and shared with me all of the incredible things that people associate with the South: delicious food, hospitality, graciousness, and manners. I took with me those life lessons and experiences when I moved to New York City for college, and later when I started my business.

A fish out of water, I found myself longing for Southern accents and sensibilities during my first year in the city. When other college students were out at clubs, I was in my dorm room watching reruns of *Designing Women*. Away from home, I developed a new appreciation for the Southern way of life in which I was raised. I re-read classics by great Southern writers and researched artists native to the low country. Eventually I traveled to Savannah, Georgia, where I felt reborn into the culture and customs I had heard about from my grandparents.

After my visit to Savannah, I committed myself to covering, supporting, and promoting Southern artists on my website. People seem to gravitate toward these makers because there is a sense of history, tradition, and sometimes mystery to their pieces that you don't often find in work from other parts of the country. They have a deep respect for, admiration of, and interest in the past. In Charleston, there are young artists revisiting the printmaking techniques used by their great-grandparents. In Athens, there are incredible ceramicists using glazes and practices handed down from older generations. And across the greater Southern landscape, there is no shortage of enthusiastic and talented makers embracing the traditions of their local communities and giving them a modern spin.

Jennifer Causey has earned the admiration of just about every community of makers I know. She approaches each artist with a sense of wonder and respect and has a way of documenting them and their processes that truly lets their skills and dedication shine. I'm so glad she's chosen to shine a light on this incredible region and its talented makers. I'm confident that their work and their stories, captured so beautifully in these pages, will continue to inspire generations to come.

Preface

·◈·

Jennifer Causey

When I finished my first book, *Brooklyn Makers*, I knew it wasn't
the end. The makers project is a work in progress for me. This is a
wonderful thing. It means that there will continue to be more artisans to
discover, and more places that are celebrating creativity and craftsmanship.
For this, my second book, I decided to head down South. I grew up
in Georgia and have many fond memories of a childhood spent enjoying
the outdoors, playing in creeks and climbing trees. I'd been living
in New York City for more than ten years, and I was looking forward to
returning to my roots.

The South is known for its distinct culture and history, customs
and cuisine. It has a proud tradition of craftsmanship, and many of its
cities are undergoing a tremendous creative renaissance in almost every
realm. I couldn't wait to learn more. Indeed, the most challenging aspect
of the project was narrowing my focus. The greater South consists of
sixteen states. In this volume, I stick to four: Tennessee, North Carolina,
South Carolina, and Georgia. They all have personal significance for
me in that they are close to where I grew up, and they all have thriving
"maker cultures" in their cities and outlying areas.

As I began my research, one of the most exciting parts was just
being out on the open road. Driving through the stunning landscapes to
visit the makers' studios, workshops, and kitchens, there was so much
to take in! Wide-open spaces, acres and acres of farmland, charming small
towns. On my way to visit Quintin Middleton of Middleton Made Knives
in South Carolina, I pulled over to photograph a beautiful field of cotton.
These are things you just don't see living in New York City.

On another occasion, driving to the rural town of Sparta to see
Megan Fowler, the letterpress printmaker of Brown Parcel Press, I passed

by the most amazing roadside stands selling boiled peanuts, peaches, and jams of all sorts. Megan was one of the first people I photographed for *Southern Makers*, and, like so many of my subjects, she was incredibly hospitable. She made me feel right at home, introducing me to her mother, husband, and young daughter, and to the lovely Southern life she has cultivated. Walking around her land was magical, as she enthusiastically described the farm and I got to meet all the animals she cares for...including her happy pigs, lazing in the mud. It was such a pleasure to see how much being a part of (and giving back to) her community means to her. I was blown away as well by the space in which she works: a former general store built in the 1920s that is now on her family's farm. The old building is quintessentially Southern, with its weathered wooden front porch and vintage Coca-Cola signage. It was inspiring to see someone so committed to craftsmanship, ethical practices, and quality: on the farm, in her letterpress studio, and in life.

Yet another memorable experience was visiting my old friend and fellow photographer Rinne Allen in Athens, Georgia. I went to college in Athens, so it holds a special place in my heart, and I enjoy having an excuse to go back, especially when it also involves an opportunity to see Rinne. Just outside her studio is a gorgeous garden with wandering paths and a meandering creek. These natural surroundings are a major influence on her photography, and I always feel renewed and energized after visiting her workspace. Rinne can talk for hours about her community and how inspired she is by other makers. It is so nice to spend time with her and walk and talk about all things creative.

Traveling to Nashville, Tennessee, was another highlight of this project. The growing metropolis boasts a strong sense of community, and its musical history—from country to blues and rock and roll—is apparent everywhere. There is a very distinct Nashville style, and it involves denim. Even in the middle of the Southern summer, everyone remains very committed to wearing their jeans. It was fun and enlightening to get a behind-the-scenes look at what makes great denim at the shop and studio of Carrie and Matt Eddmenson of Imogene + Willie. (They will tell you it's all about the fit.) Like a number of the places I photographed in the South, the couple chose to renovate an old structure rather than build something new. Their beautiful factory and store on 12th Avenue South was originally the Granny White Service

Station. Carrie and Matt are heavily embedded in and dedicated to the rising creative community in Nashville. Their store supports many local makers, including Otis James, and they recently undertook a collaboration with Asheville jeweler Hannah Ferrara of Another Feather.

It was deeply gratifying to see so many makers in the South forming communities and actively supporting one another. This was especially evident in Charleston, South Carolina. Everyone seems to know everyone else, and there is an overwhelming sense of excitement surrounding food and craft. When I visited Brooks Reitz of Jack Rudy Cocktail Co., his hospitality was also at the forefront. I had arranged to photograph him early in the morning at his home (at the time, his living room was also used as his packaging facility), and he made me coffee and even offered to cook me breakfast; we readily bonded over our mutual love for beautiful cookbooks. Photographing Brooks felt like photographing an old friend, even though we had just met. I was honored to get a sneak peek at one of his new products, Small Batch Grenadine, and he proudly told me about his suppliers and all the work that had gone into developing it.

Photographing and talking with the artisans featured in this book reminded me how much I love the South. The Southern way of life—slowing down, sharing stories, taking pride in your craft—is truly infectious, and incredibly inspiring. I hope you will enjoy spending time with these makers as much as I did.

Makers Map

·⊰◇⊱·

Illustrated by Becca Barnet of Sisal and Tow

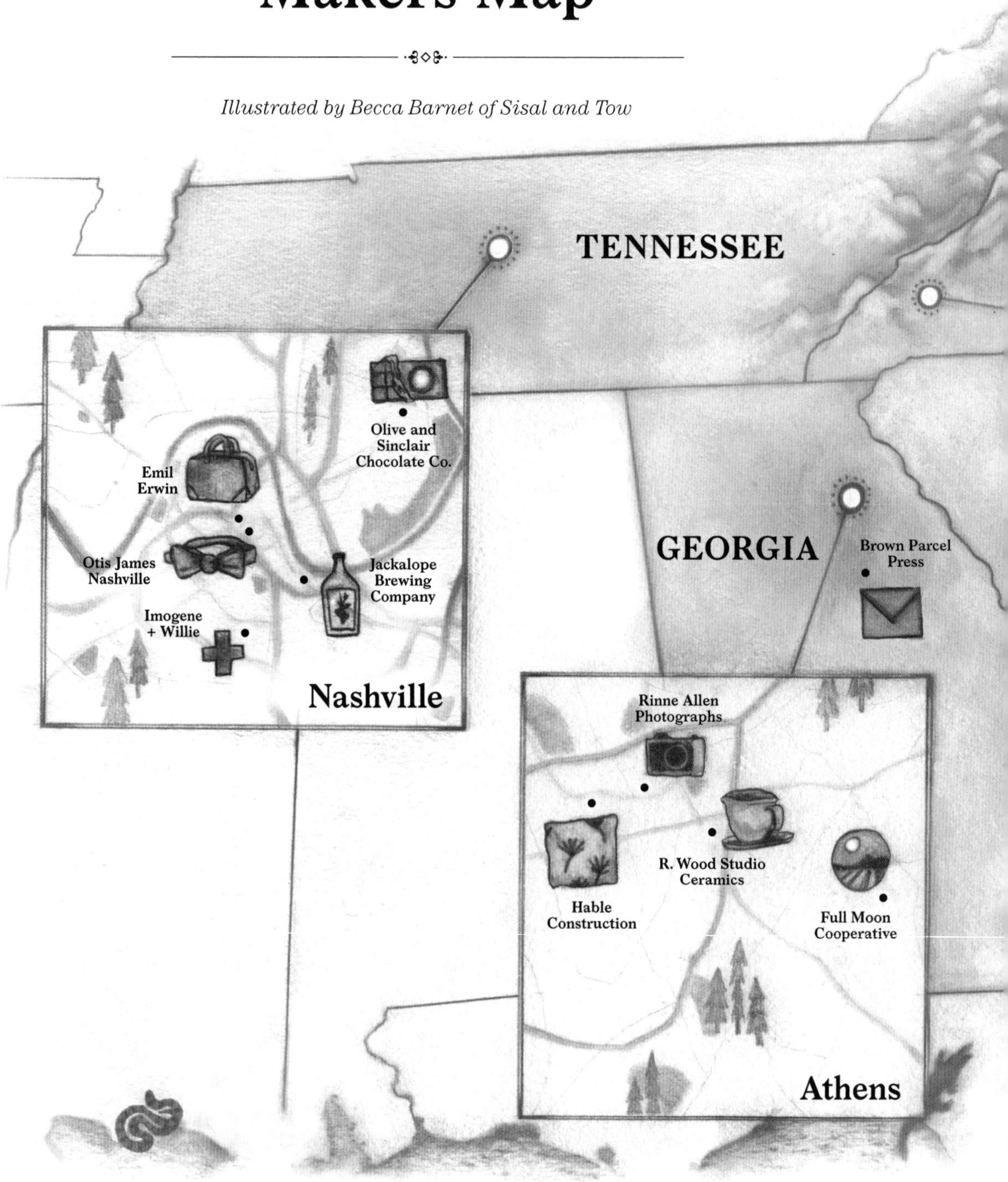

TENNESSEE

Olive and
Sinclair
Chocolate Co.

Emil
Erwin

Otis James
Nashville

Jackalope
Brewing
Company

Imogene
+ Willie

Nashville

GEORGIA

Brown Parcel
Press

Rinne Allen
Photographs

R. Wood Studio
Ceramics

Hable
Construction

Full Moon
Cooperative

Athens

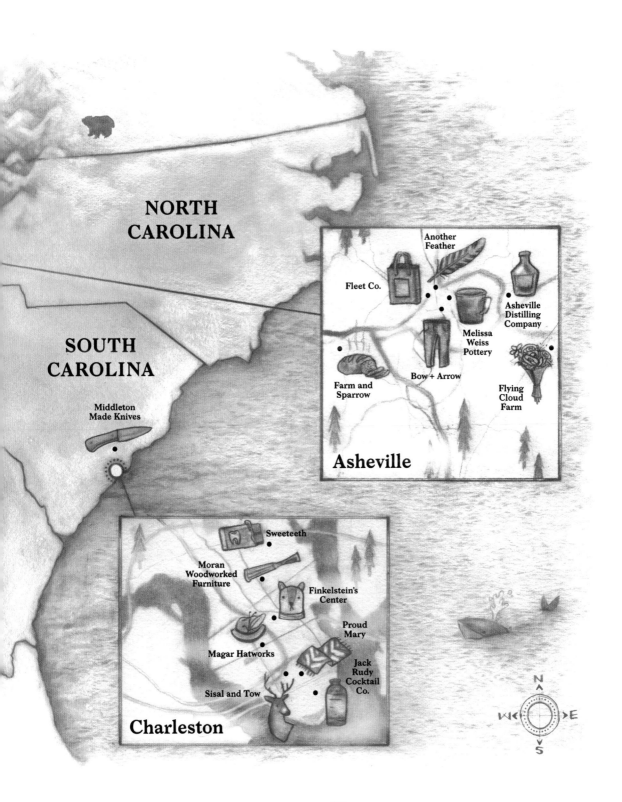

NORTH
CAROLINA

SOUTH
CAROLINA

Middleton
Made Knives

Asheville

Another
Feather

Fleet Co.

Asheville
Distilling
Company

Melissa
Weiss
Pottery

Farm and
Sparrow

Bow + Arrow

Flying
Cloud
Farm

Charleston

Sweeteeth

Moran
Woodworked
Furniture

Finkelstein's
Center

Proud
Mary

Magar Hatworks

Jack
Rudy
Cocktail
Co.

Sisal and Tow

N
W E
S

TENNESSEE

Bounded by the Mississippi River to the west and the Appalachian Mountains to the east, Tennessee has much natural beauty to boast about. It is also home to bustling metropolises, from Memphis to Nashville. Nashville, the state capital, is at the center of the South's creative boom. Popularly known as Music City for its rich history of rock and roll, blues, and country, it is also a hub for celebrated designers, chefs, and even brewers, and is the embodiment of new Southern cool. This is evident in the acclaimed denim of Imogene + Willie, the carefully crafted textiles of Otis James, and the highly sought-after leather pieces of Emil Erwin. Further, the mouthwatering creations of Olive and Sinclair Chocolate Co. and Jackalope Brewing Company provide a taste of Southern tradition and experimentation, a hallmark combination of new and old makers that makes Nashville so special.

Otis James Nashville

who — **Otis James**
location — **Nashville, Tennessee**

Located in Nashville's historic downtown, the studio of craftsman Otis James is in the creative complex of Marathon Village, named for the century-old Marathon Motor Works building. Once a car factory, the landmark structure is now a central point of the city's artistic community (it is also home to Otis's former studiomate Emil Congdon of Emil Erwin). From the lofty, brick-and-beam space, Otis proudly makes custom ties and hats for his label, Otis James Nashville.

Born in California, Otis was raised in Knoxville, Tennessee. Following a move back to the West Coast to study film, he returned to the South in 2009, making Nashville his home. Inspired by the creative boom of the city in art, food, and fashion, Otis set out to make custom clothing. He apprenticed with a master tailor and later worked in a tuxedo shop while building his business. After a year of making ties on commission, he approached the local retailer Imogene + Willie about carrying his line. Known for his rich material palette—from waxed canvas to camel hair to tweed—and careful attention to every detail, he has gained national recognition as part of the new guard of tailoring. Otis has expanded his offerings to include neckties, bow ties, and caps (the Brawler, Slugger, and Captain). Each classic piece is finished off with an individually numbered and hand-printed label, proclaiming: Otis James Nashville.

Located in the landmark Marathon Motor Works building, Otis's industrial studio was formerly shared with Emil Erwin (note the suspenders on the following spread). Here, Otis dons his signature Brawler cap, also featured in his retro-style "How to Tie a Tie" instructional poster.

How has living in the South influenced your work? Living in the South has allowed me to slow down, tune out a good part of what everyone else is doing, and focus on my own methods and ideas. While it's very easy to access new trends and fads down here, it's just as easy to seek inspiration from other aspects of life.

Describe the importance of "Nashville" in your business name. The business name is my name and where I work. When I was in college, I sold cheap suits, and it really irked me that all these poorly made suits would put fashion-centric cities on their labels, like Milan, New York, or Paris, merely for the association. The "Nashville" on my label means that it's designed and made in Nashville.

Where did you learn your craft? When I first moved to Nashville, I apprenticed at a tailor shop to learn alterations. However, I learned my craft on my own. I'm always studying how garments are made. When I go into a clothing store, I'm looking at all the seams and folds and curves and trying to work out the process in my head. So I studied ties and caps, took them apart, experimented, and made endless prototypes.

Why did you decide to make ties and hats over other products? Making ties was never something I set out to do. I truly fell into it, and I couldn't be more grateful. I was asked by a coworker at the tux shop to make two ties for Father's Day gifts. They were a success, and she suggested I make custom ties for weddings. Within a month, I got my first commission, and from there word spread that I was a custom tie maker.

Caps are a different story. I've always had a passion for caps. I bought my first tweed ivy cap when I was fourteen and wore it everywhere for the next twelve years. It was really tough for me to take it apart to study it and draft a new pattern. If I could only make one item for the rest of my life, I could probably be content just making caps.

What is the most satisfying part of your making process? Delivering a finished piece to a customer. My obsession is with connection between source and destination. I create for people, not for myself. So when I see the excitement and satisfaction someone experiences from something I've made, it brings me great joy. The work can get tiring, but the payoff never gets old.

Emil Erwin

who — **Emil Congdon**
location — **Nashville, Tennessee**

Emil Congdon started handcrafting leather bags out of his garage while working full time at a computer retailer in 2008. He grew up in the Tennessee mountain town of Erwin, which is also his grandmother's maiden name. In homage to his heritage (family and place), when he took the leap to start his own business, he named it Emil Erwin.

Emil is primarily self-taught; he worked as a high-end auto upholsterer for several years and that was where he honed his sewing skills and laid the groundwork for Emil Erwin. He also embraced early trial and error, a critical part of any making process. Today, he crafts each of his products by hand using heavy leather, waxed canvas, or both.

The entire collection is patterned, cut, sewn, and assembled in a large warehouse studio in Marathon Village. Emil and his wife, Leslie, design all the products in the line. They have two employees who assist in production, but Emil does all the final assembly himself, acting as chief craftsman. In 2009, Emil Erwin collaborated on a successful custom line with the Nashville denim designers Imogene + Willie.

The celebrated designer believes in quality without compromise, and in using the best materials, tools, and techniques to make a superior product— one that will stand the test of time. Each Emil Erwin product carries the craftsman's pledge: It is guaranteed for life.

34

Emil's handcrafted bags, including the Erwin Briefcase, are made with top-quality hides from Chicago's Horween Leather Company. Carefully constructed with solid copper rivets and stainless steel brackets, the products can also be monogrammed with the hot stamp embosser.

What do you enjoy most about living in Nashville? Nashville is more a town than a city. It's big enough to keep you occupied, but small enough that you know your mailman.

How has the South influenced your work? The South embraces a slower—not to be confused with lazier—pace. You really have a chance to soak in your surroundings and appreciate the influences your environment has to offer. Sometimes it is a bit slow for my taste, but it lends itself to care and attention that might be lost if we were racing around with our heads down.

How did you become interested in leatherworking? There was a saddle shop in my hometown of Erwin, Tennessee, that I would visit as a child. I would weave through the hanging belts and bridles. Something about the smell and texture grabbed hold of me and never let go. Leather is such an amazing product. Its durability and versatility are unmatched.

What was the moment you decided to start your business? Leslie and I decided to do it full time after we were featured in *Garden and Gun* magazine in late 2010. We had such a strong response that I couldn't fulfill the orders and maintain my day job. So I quit. It was completely liberating and horrifying at the same time. We had just had our second child and I was walking away from a steady salary and benefits. But I had wanted to run my own business since I was a kid. (I tried to open a skate shop in my grandmother's basement.) I take my work very personally and have only felt fulfilled since starting this business.

What is the best part of being your own boss? I always completely invest myself into my job. It's great to know that all of my efforts are going toward building a legacy for my kids and not just lining the pockets of some corporation.

What is the most satisfying part of your making process? It is all so satisfying. Designing, creating, and selling. I mention selling because that is the point when someone lets you know that they also believe in what you are doing.

Jackalope Brewing Company

who — **Bailey Spaulding**
Robyn Virball
location — **Nashville, Tennessee**

"Believe in yourself." As Bailey Spaulding and Robyn Virball were starting Jackalope Brewing Company in 2009, this became their unofficial motto. (The jackalope is a creature that is half-rabbit, half-antelope, and entirely nonexistent.) Based in Nashville, the very real Jackalope brewery produces handcrafted ales and hosts special events such as Docktoberfest (Octoberfest on the brewery's loading dock). The taproom opened in May 2011, and distribution in the city began in January 2012.

Bailey and Robyn met during college and became fast friends. After law school, Bailey, a longtime home brewer, decided to pursue her dream of starting a brewery, and Robyn came on board. They wrote a business plan, found investors, signed a lease—and Jackalope was born. Bailey is the brewmaster; she took a course in commercial brewing during the business development phase, and running the brewing equipment has provided plenty of on-the-job training in mechanical engineering. Robyn is in charge of the "front of house" operations. Jackalope's taproom offers rotating beers that change every month, often featuring local and seasonal ingredients. For Bailey and brewer Steve Wright, experimentation with recipes keeps the brewing process fun and engaging. Jackalope also pairs certain beers with local nonprofits, with a percentage of the proceeds benefiting that organization. Bailey and Robyn plan to keep growing at a sustainable rate while holding on to their original values. Believe it.

Bailey and Robyn have been providing Nashville with Jackalope craft beer since 2009. From the brewery to the taproom, making and enjoying their product is a hands-on, around-the-clock process.

I love the suspense and the idea of creating something that's never been made before.

What do you enjoy most about living in Nashville? *Bailey:* So much! Obviously, I love the music. There are very talented people everywhere you look, and everyone is so passionate about what is happening in the city. There is an amazing feeling of community because we all believe in each other's endeavors. I also have learned that I love fried pickles and Goo Goo Clusters.

What was the moment you decided to start your business? How did you partner up? *Bailey:* I had thought about it for a long time and was having a bit of a crisis around the time of law school graduation. Then Robyn said she'd start the brewery with me, so at least one other person thought it was a good enough idea to put herself at stake. We had lots of "this is really happening" moments. Robyn moved down here, we wrote the business plan, we got investors, we signed our lease. The next thing you know, you're no longer "thinking of starting a brewery"; you actually run one.

Robyn: As for partnering up, Bailey always says that of all the people who'd claim, "You want to start a brewery? I'll totally do it with you!" I was the only one who actually did it. What's the expression? 99 percent of success is just showing up!

Where does your business name come from? *Bailey:* I believed in jackalopes growing up. A family friend who was a taxidermist would tell me stories about how they were nocturnal and only

lived in Montana. It all seemed very plausible. Years later a friend gave me a T-shirt with a jackalope on it that read "Believe in Yourself." As we were starting the brewery, and going down a path a bit less traveled, it turned into our unofficial motto.

What hours do you keep? *Bailey:* Beer knows no weekend, as they say, and you have to be ready for any situation. In the summer when it's 130 degrees in the brewery, we brew overnight to minimize the heat hallucinations. You have to be very dedicated to your job because it becomes an inextricable part of your identity. It's a good thing we have plenty of beer around.

What is the most satisfying part of your making process? *Bailey:* The most relieving moment is coming back in the morning after you brew and seeing the liquid in the blow-off bucket bubbling away. It means that the fermentation is going and the yeast is converting the sugar into alcohol and carbon dioxide. Also, who doesn't like bubbles? I also love the very first sip of a brand-new brew. I love the suspense and the idea of creating something that's never been made before.

Robyn: In the taproom, I've encountered people who come in claiming not to like beer, and then walk out with a growler because they love our product. It's been a long road getting here, so it's really satisfying when people like what we do.

Imogene + Willie

who — **Carrie Eddmenson**
Matt Eddmenson
location — **Nashville, Tennessee**

At the Imogene + Willie store in Nashville, Carrie and Matt Eddmenson design and sell their distinctive clothing line, featuring jeans and work shirts and the occasional dress or jacket. The pair honed their denim skills while working at Carrie's family's denim business in Henderson, Kentucky. When that business closed due to the surge of overseas manufacturing, they decided to launch their own brand. Their personal story goes back much further. The pair met when they were only ten years old. They married in 2006 and opened their business in 2009. Clearly, they make a great team.

Carrie and Matt had always imagined that their future business would be housed in a former gas station. When they discovered the Granny White Service Station in Nashville—a building that exuded history and was vacant and available—they knew it was the place. They renovated the space, transforming it into a factory, office, and retail store. In a few short years, Imogene + Willie grew into a brand with a cult following, known for its careful attention to fit. Perhaps less tangible but equally important to their brand are the ideals of family, community, and relationships with those who make their products. For the couple—and for Imogene + Willie—the old service station on 12th Avenue South feels as comfortable as, well, a favorite pair of jeans.

For Carrie and Matt, a
little alteration can go a long
way—from fitting a jean
to converting a gas station
into a handsome shop and
office space. In the store,
patterns hang from the
ceiling, old receipts line the
bathroom walls, and vintage
Americana abounds.

What brought you to Nashville? The gas station. We fell in love with the building, so we moved to Nashville to open shop.

Describe your store space and its history. The store space was originally the Granny White Service Station when 12th Avenue South was still a dirt road. The founder's children still live in town and have shared with us stories of their dad's old station. We have the original sign on loan from them. When we renovated the space, we pulled out the ceiling and thousands of receipts fell out that had been used for insulation. We ended up wallpapering the bathroom with the receipts, and still today, people recognize the many names from years ago.

Where does your business name come from? It is named after Carrie's grandparents— Willie and Imogene—and in honor of all of our family and the work ethic that they instilled in us.

Do you have a daily routine? Since we have the pleasure of being both business partners and husband and wife, we take turns making the coffee when we first wake up and then begin to return emails from bed. Carrie and about half of our staff work from our offsite office on strategic planning, media, graphic design, production, finance, and more. Matt heads to the shop to work with our design team and to create (and re-create) the retail space, making sure the curation is fresh every week. We come home, work until we go to sleep, and then do it all over again.

What is the best part of being your own boss? You can wake up every morning and, if need be, redefine.

What are your influences? Family, community, relationships with the people who make our products, and simple, quality curation. Less is more.

What is the most satisfying part of your making process? The opportunity to actually dream it, design it, and make it in the shop.

Olive and Sinclair Chocolate Co.

who — **Scott Witherow**
location — **Nashville, Tennessee**

Sample a bite of Olive and Sinclair's Bourbon Nib Brittle, and you will be transported to the South. Made with cacao aged in bourbon barrels from Southern distillers, the brittle features subtle notes of apple, cherry, and oak, ending with notes of bourbon. It is just one of a line of confections created by self-taught chocolatier Scott Witherow.

The South influences everything Scott does at Olive and Sinclair. Born and raised in Nashville, he spent years in the restaurant industry, working in kitchens in London, Chicago, and Birmingham before returning to his hometown. Intrigued by the science of chocolate, he experimented with roasting beans and tested small batches on family and friends. Eventually he came up with what he dubbed "Southern artisan chocolate": chocolates crafted bean-to-bar with uniquely Southern ingredients and methods. They stone-grind their cacao with pure brown sugar. Their white chocolate incorporates buttermilk, a Southern staple. And Scott uses the smokehouse at the famous Benton's Smoky Mountain Country Hams to smoke the cacao nibs for his Smoked Nib Brittle. The attention to handcrafted detail extends to the wrapping and packaging of the bars, which is done on site.

Founded in 2009, the business made a name for itself quickly. (Gwyneth Paltrow discovered Olive and Sinclair while she was filming a movie in town and raved about the chocolates on her website.) Scott remains true to his original inspirations: a love of cacao and its complexities, and a fascination with the process of making good chocolate.

Scott's chocolate bars are manifestations of the sweet Southern life. He uses buttermilk and molasses, staples of the South, and commissions local artists to illustrate and print the wrappers.

How has living in the South influenced your work? Everything about the South influences what we do. We try to use what we have, a sort of forced tradition of Southern cuisine—from used bourbon barrels to access to great smokehouses to buttermilk—all of which have helped define and refine our "Southern artisan chocolate."

Did you have another career before starting Olive and Sinclair? I have been in restaurants, in one way or another, since I was fifteen. I tried the insurance business for a while, made a brief attempt at selling real estate, and was a janitor and a mover for a bit—all not for me. But I do love working with my hands, and getting paid to work with and make chocolate and other confections is a real dream come true.

What was the moment you decided to start your business? I have always dreamed of having my own business. When I was flying back from England, I made a list of what I wanted to do. Chocolate was on the list. It was years later, after dabbling in the molecular side of cooking, that I became interested in the science of chocolate.

I started reading about it, and subsequently ran across a bean-to-bar chocolate maker in Canada. I bought close to a pound of chocolate that night and ate every bit of it. I didn't know how to make chocolate but decided then and there that I was going to start a chocolate company.

What makes your chocolate distinctive? Our chocolate is different on many levels. First we only use cacao beans and brown sugar. The sorghum and molasses combine with the cacao for a robust flavor unique to our chocolate. Also, our buttermilk white chocolate is about as unique as it sounds. A Southern staple, the buttermilk provides a tang that balances the overt sweet and fattiness of the white chocolate. We also pride ourselves on our packaging, giving our chocolate a personable and Southern quality (the art on our wrappers was originally drawn and printed by Nashville hands).

What is the best part of working with your hands? Having chocolate constantly all over them! I just really enjoy making things. Time flies by, and then the best part is hearing about or seeing someone enjoying it.

NORTH CAROLINA

With a long history of furniture making, one of the state's key economies, North Carolina is built on craftsmanship and particularly emblematizes the creative life of the South. The mountain metropolis of Asheville—an Art Deco mecca—is especially well known for its thriving arts community. The scenic Blue Ridge Parkway passes through the city and the famed eight-thousand-acre Biltmore Estate is its most notable landmark. Home to more than thirty art galleries, Asheville also boasts lively downtown music and culinary scenes. This rich, vibrant area is the perfect operating ground for many of the state's esteemed makers, including Another Feather and Fleet Co., whose owners are a husband-and-wife team and craft (respectively) jewelry and leather goods. Melissa Weiss Pottery and Bow + Arrow both work out of the burgeoning River Arts District. At the city's edge and beyond, Farm and Sparrow bakery, Asheville Distilling Company, and the Flying Cloud Farm are also contributing to the state's creative renaissance.

Another Feather

who — **Hannah Ferrara**
location — **Asheville, North Carolina**

Hannah Ferrara and her husband, Malcolm Smitley (of Fleet Co.), have converted the front room of their home into a shared studio. Although they practice different crafts, the inspiration-filled space reflects their similar sensibilities and work ethics and succeeds functionally and aesthetically.

A frequent traveler, Hannah grew up in North Carolina and is influenced by her voyages (near and far), the Blue Ridge Mountains, and an appreciation for well-made objects and heirlooms. Hannah studied metals and jewelry design, as well as textiles and fibers, and uses traditional metalsmithing techniques and tools to create her pieces. Employing sustainable practices, she works with recycled metals and occasionally incorporates natural objects such as antlers and rough stones and minerals. For her everyday and one-of-a-kind adornments (including necklaces, earrings, bracelets, and rings), she carefully crafts each detail while embracing the beautiful imperfections of her handcrafted process.

Her work is inspired by the South, reflecting the belief that it's always a little rugged even when refined. When Hannah's not traveling to a new city, she takes advantage of her surroundings and gets out of her studio (often with her husband) to walk, bike, and picnic near the woods or river.

Hannah's sunlit home studio is filled with collections from her travels (which are often incorporated into her work), sketches for a new line, and tools and cuttings for her jewelry production.

How has living in the South influenced your work? The South is very narrative-heavy. We love stories, and meanings, and the history behind things. It's also always a little rugged even when refined. Western North Carolina and the Appalachian Mountains are particularly heavy in traditional skills and crafts. Handcrafted items are important here, and Southerners place a certain amount of pride and value in beautiful, well-made objects, especially those with a story. Living around these mountains and the folklore surrounding them has certainly influenced my work.

Where does your business name come from? Since I was a girl, I pick up any lost feather I come across. While on the coast, I'd gather the feathers of seagulls and herons; in the Piedmont, I'd stuff bluebird and pheasant feathers in my pockets; now in the mountains, I find plenty of wild turkey feathers. The name embodies my love for collecting and the natural world.

Where do you source the materials used in your work? Almost everything I use is sourced domestically, aside from a few raw stones. I usually collect natural objects in the woods close by or on visits to the coast, but I've also been known to carry a few back home with me from trips abroad.

Do you listen to music while you work? I love just listening to the rhythm of my hammering, the filing of edges, the flick of my torch.

What is the most significant investment you've made in your business? Staying still long enough to establish a somewhat concrete studio.

What is the most satisfying part of your making process? There's nothing quite like finishing a piece and then slipping it on to admire. There is a sense of fulfillment in seeing a design or idea come to completion.

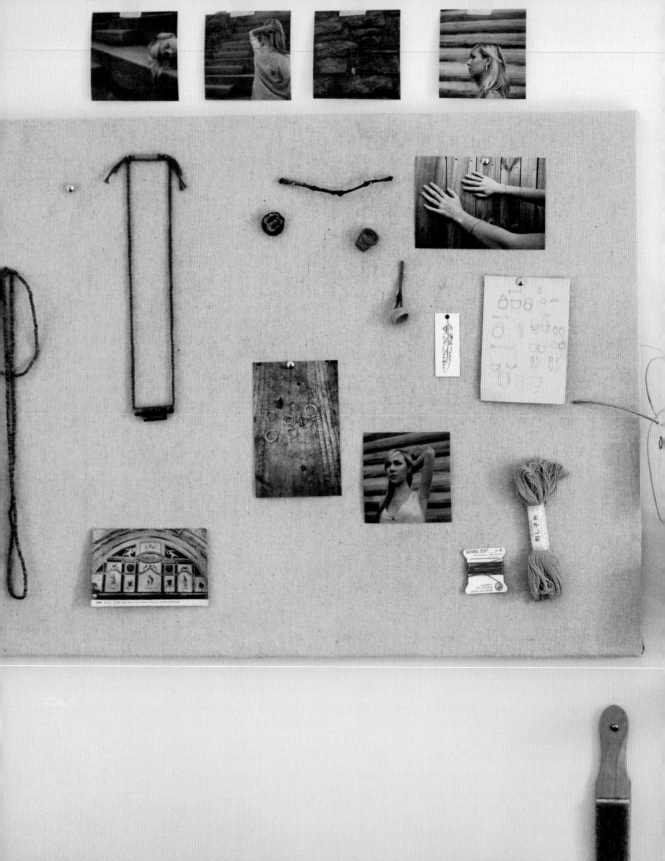

Fleet Co.

who — **Malcolm Smitley**
location — **Asheville, North Carolina**

A simple, utilitarian wallet. A woman's bag. Malcolm Smitley was looking for everyday leather items for himself and his wife (Hannah Ferrara of Another Feather) and ended up making them himself. Thus began Fleet Co., a line of leather goods produced in the couple's small studio in the front room of their home in Asheville.

Growing up, Malcolm nurtured a passion for making, including a love of food and cooking. He attended culinary school and currently works full time as a chef, but he spends much of his free time working on Fleet Co. The hands-on approach is evident in his leatherwork. A self-taught craftsman, Malcolm hand-dyes all his own leathers—on the front porch, when the weather allows—and hand stitches each piece. The leather is all sourced in North America. From Malcolm and Hannah's shared appreciation of a natural, functional aesthetic has come a line of well-made items—some, such as Fleet's leather-covered flask, with a uniquely Southern point of view.

Best of all, the items are built to last: made to be bought, used, and then passed down to the next generation.

On the front porch of his home in downtown Asheville, Malcolm dyes leather for a new project. In his studio, he handcrafts his specialty goods, including Southern-inspired, leather-wrapped flasks.

67

How has living in the South influenced your work? Folks in the South really care about tradition, and they appreciate well-made items. They also value things they can use every day and that will last for years. In this way, the South has influenced the utilitarian goods I make and the rugged yet somewhat refined style of my work. My collection of leather-covered stainless steel flasks was inspired by Southerners' love of good whiskey.

Where does your business name come from? The word *fleet* is often used in the nautical sense, but I love that it embodies the action of movement. For the last six years, I traveled from place to place, and while I've spent this last year in one place, it reminds me to keep moving forward.

Do you have a daily routine? I work full time as a chef, so most days it's hard to have an official routine. When I have a full day to spend in the workshop, though, I wake up extremely early and begin with a cup of coffee, breakfast, and sketching out designs. Then I typically jump right into making. Hannah and I try to take an official break for a real meal if we are both working in the studio. Then orders are packaged up, emails are sent, and with the free time left in the day I usually head out to shoot bow and arrow or take a long bike ride.

How did you become interested in leatherworking? I always loved the idea of working with leather and making utilitarian goods, but knew nothing about it. When I moved to the mountains, I found a strong culture of making and had access to hides from a local leather supply company. In the winter these mountains get cold, so having something to do with your hands is really helpful to keep your mind moving when stuck indoors. I started making some samples and it just clicked.

What is the best part of working with your hands? I've always worked with my hands, so there's something nostalgic about it. My dad worked with wood and as a kid I would help him build tables and other items we needed for the house. I love using my skills to create a functional and beautiful object that will last year after year and am so grateful I'm able to work with my hands on a daily basis in both of my crafts.

Melissa Weiss Pottery

who — **Melissa Weiss**
location — **Asheville, North Carolina**

A large window overlooking the French Broad River brings beautiful light to Melissa Weiss's pottery studio in the Wedge, an old industrial warehouse in the popular River Arts District in Asheville. The studio is, not surprisingly, covered in clay—often clay that comes directly out of the Southern ground. Melissa uses clay that she digs from her own plot of land in Arkansas. "Wild clay," she calls it. Her designs feature organic forms and imagery inspired by nature. Trees and leaves abound.

Melissa took up pottery when her daughter was three months old. After her first class, she was hooked. Working with clay gave her a much-needed outlet from the intensity of her role as a new mother. Wood-firing gave her a new way to finish her pots, as well as the aesthetic challenge she needed to grow. For her, the wood kiln is a revitalizing experience in which every firing is different, every pot is unique, and the process cannot be entirely controlled. This is where she finds motivation.

Melissa was born in New York, then spent half of her life in Northern California and the other half in New York City. She graduated from the School of Visual Arts with a degree in photography. On her first foray into the South, in 2002, she bought some land in Arkansas simply because it was so affordable. In 2005 she went to Asheville to house-sit for a friend. She has been there ever since, finding Asheville—with its supportive community and camaraderie among artists—the perfect place to raise her daughter and make pottery.

Using "wild clay" from her land in the Ozarks, Melissa creates wood-fired ceramic cups, plates, bowls, and other housewares. Her whimsical, clay-covered studio overlooks the train tracks and the French Broad River.

What do you enjoy most about living in Asheville? I love the mountains, the French Broad River, and the weather. I love the small-town feeling of recognizing people in the grocery store. That doesn't happen in big cities. It seems easy to get along here. It's calm.

How has the South influenced your work? I didn't even make pots before I moved to the South, so it has influenced every aspect. I use clay right out of the Southern ground. I have been almost exclusively influenced by the large population of potters in western North Carolina, especially the wood-fired potters.

Describe your studio. I work out of the Clayspace Co-op in a large old industrial warehouse called the Wedge in the River Arts District. It is next to the train tracks and along the French Broad River, full of artists. My studio has large windows that look out on the train and river. I love my studio and the area. It is a very supportive community for my pottery making. Within the area, there are dozens of other potters and we all help each other out.

Describe the aesthetic of your work. I don't try to "clean up" or cover up the fact that my pots are handmade. I make my clay partly from my land in the Ozarks and the nature of the wild clay has a component that commercial clays lack. It's alive. It is imperfect and slightly unpredictable. I try to make pots that don't look out of place in the natural world. I use a muted palette. I decorate with iron oxide and also by scratching through the slip to the dark clay underneath. I use simple geometric patterns and plant forms.

What is the most satisfying part of your making process? Since I am involved in every step, each part is equally satisfying. I dig the clay, make the clay, make the pots, make the glazes and slips, decorate, and fire. Each of these steps is an integral part of the finished pot. The finished pot was a pile of dirt on my land in Arkansas just months before.

What are your influences? Margaret Kilgallen, my grandma (and watching her cook), old enamel dishes, African and Mexican sculptures and patterns, old children's picture books.

Bow + Arrow

who — **Anna Toth**
location — **Asheville, North Carolina**

Clothing designer Anna Toth started Bow + Arrow in 2010. The apparel line includes women's jeans as well as made-to-measure basics such as overalls, shorts, skirts, and dresses. Other Bow + Arrow items include floppy sun hats and a utilitarian, unisex work apron with all the pockets one could desire.

Custom high-waisted denim is a large part of Anna's business; she hand-drafts a pattern for each client so that each garment fits perfectly. Bow + Arrow has a strong commitment to creating a 100 percent domestic product whenever possible. All of the denim Anna uses is from cotton that is grown, milled, and finished in the United States. Its wearers inevitably find it versatile, beloved, and useful.

Anna has lived the majority of her life in the South. Born in Charleston, South Carolina, and raised in Lexington, Kentucky, she spent six years in San Francisco, California, and a brief time in Tennessee before settling in Asheville. Anna's studio is upstairs from Melissa Weiss Pottery in the Wedge building. Located in the heart of the River Arts District, the studio's wood, brick, and sunlight reflects the all-American appeal of Bow + Arrow denim.

Anna cuts denim to custom patterns, prepares leather for made-to-measure belts, and displays a selection of finished wares in her Wedge Studios workspace, part of Asheville's celebrated River Arts District.

What brought you back to the South?
I came back four years ago because I missed four perfect seasons, genuine character, a lush garden, proximity to family, green everywhere, front and back porches, waterfalls, cicadas, and fireflies, in no particular order.

How has living in the South influenced your work? There is a vibrant craft heritage tradition in Southern Appalachia, and a real understanding of hard work and simple living. I can't think of anything more suited for hard work and simple living than a good pair of jeans.

Describe your studio. Five hundred square feet of hardwood, brick, and sunlight in the heart of the River Arts District. My neighbors are lovely and inspiring people. I can hear the train go by several times a day, and sometimes it shakes the building. When I'm working at night, I hear people enjoying the brewery downstairs, and smell the food trucks serving up deliciousness.

What was the moment you decided to start your business? Shortly after returning to Asheville, I was working in a neighboring community called Sandy Mush. The lady I worked for had a scroll-making business,

and a Mountain Inn and Healing Sanctuary. It was while I was painting the finials of a scroll that I thought to myself, "If they can make enough money selling scrolls to hire me on, then I should probably make clothes."

What is the most satisfying part of your making process? I love the whole making process, but the finished product is my favorite. I put a lot into the patternmaking for each client, and am a stickler for detail when I'm driving my machines. When a client puts on their new jeans, it's like a moment of truth. It's extremely gratifying to see that work pay off, and to know that I've made someone really happy. I think the client and I are both high from it for the day.

What is the best part of being your own boss? The risk-and-reward relationship. It's dangerous and exciting, and therefore deeply gratifying.

What are your influences? Books like *Native Funk and Flash*, *Handmade Houses*, and anything published by Lloyd Kahn. Leathered hands and faces. Things that were built to last. Canoe trips and meals by the campfire. Life and death and the stuff in between.

Farm and Sparrow

who — **David Bauer**
location — **Candler, North Carolina**

Wisconsin native David Bauer lives and works on one acre of land in Candler, North Carolina, just outside of Asheville. He runs his business out of his renovated garage-turned-bakery, complete with a large wood-fired brick oven and a homemade walk-in cooler. David prides himself on baking all his breads and pastries using traditional processes with organic whole grains stone-milled on site (the mill is in a small building next door to the bakery).

A self-taught baker, David has always worked with his hands—playing music, working on farms, cooking in restaurants, carving wood, and much more. Before baking bread, he built ovens with the renowned oven builder Alan Scott, who introduced him to many small craft bakers. The bakery is a full-time/lifetime commitment, consuming twelve hours or more a day (which begin at 3:30 in the morning on market days).

Although he landed in Asheville by happenstance, he has embraced the area. He integrates Southern grains and produce into his baked goods and has created a unique and much-beloved community bakery, Farm and Sparrow.

Just outside of Asheville, the Farm and Sparrow team prepares their baked goods from the garage of David's ranch-style home. The property houses a mill and the garage-turned-bakery, complete with a walk-in cooler and wood-fired brick oven.

My hands, eyes, ears, and body are all constantly engaged with the mill, the oven, and the bread. You've got to stay dialed in.

What was the moment you decided to start your business? Starting this business was a grand accident. I had been working in restaurants, baking for chefs, building ovens, and working on farms for years. I had traveled around the country in search of the next step. Then, I was contacted by a baker in Asheville who was looking for someone to lease her wood-fired bakehouse. There was a stone mill, too. I knew that was what I wanted to be doing. I wasn't trying to start a business. I just wanted to have a space to study and learn. Farm and Sparrow grew out of those early years of intense experimentation.

Describe your workspace. I work in my garage. I live on one acre of land in Candler, which is just outside of Asheville. We have chickens, a big garden, and many young fruit trees and berry shrubs. There is a very large wood-fired brick oven built out of one of the garage doors. The floor is all brick tile. We have a couple of mixers, three tables, a wall of wooden shelves to hold the bread while it cools, and a homemade walk-in cooler. In an outbuilding right next door, our milling takes place.

What is your favorite product? A simple loaf of bread—our Market Bread. It takes so much work to make this bread. The flour is stone-ground slowly and sifted very finely until it is

so delicate, but with all of the aromas from the germ oil rubbed into it. It is such a ridiculously labor-intensive pursuit. Other bakeries just blend white flour into a bread. As long as we're making this bread, I know that I'm working toward something more than just a paycheck.

Describe your milling process. Milling our own flour makes the whole process complete for me. We work with a single variety of wheat, called Turkey wheat, and most of it is single source, meaning that we know the farm it came from and what weather that crop had. Very old grains like Turkey wheat will vary when grown in different locales. Every time there's a new crop, we have to revise our process. So we don't have a standard recipe. This is highly unusual in modern baking. It's really exciting for us. Without a mill, we would be dependent on the same mass-produced flour as everyone else.

What is the most satisfying part of your making process? The most satisfying part of my work is that my senses are engaged all the time. I get to spend my days trying to preserve the smell of wheat. So I'm always smelling flour, smelling dough, smelling bread. My hands, eyes, ears, and body are all constantly engaged with the mill, the oven, and the bread. You've got to stay dialed in. It is unlike any other job I can think of.

Asheville Distilling Company

who — **Troy Ball**
location — **Asheville, North Carolina**

Troy Ball creates small-batch, handcrafted spirits that, as she claims and others agree, "any credible moonshiner would drink himself." The Texas native and mother of three grown boys moved her family to the Blue Ridge Mountains of Asheville in 2004. Her love of moonshine, and the idea to pursue the business, was sparked by a neighbor's welcome gift: a jar of homemade hooch.

In 2010, Troy and her husband, Charlie, opened Asheville Distilling Company, founded on the so-called "keeper" whiskey (old-time moonshiners are known for keeping their best whiskey for themselves). Troy's moonshine is made from pure Appalachian spring water, locally grown white corn, and heirloom Crooked Creek Corn, a white corn that is only grown in North Carolina. She gets her supply from the nearby McEntire farm, where it has been cultivated for more than 120 years. In addition to their signature white Platinum Moonshine whiskey, the distillery offers a bourbon barrel–aged Oak Reserve and the newly released Blonde Whiskey, a smooth spirit with no burn or bite.

The distillery's current home is in a three-thousand-square-foot space located in the former Southern Railway Wheelhouse. It houses a custom-made five-thousand-liter copper still and state-of-the-art distilling equipment. The building is part of the Highland Brewing Co. and Tasting Room, which hosts live music, food, and tastings. From here, Troy pursues her commitment to distill "kinder spirits, smoother whiskeys" and to distribute this proudly Southern product across the country.

Troy inspects a pour from the custom-made copper still in the distillery's new space, located in the former Southern Railway Wheelhouse.

What do you enjoy most about living in Asheville? Asheville is a city where you can be who you want to be. You can reinvent yourself, pursue your passions, and bask in handmade art and music.

How has the South influenced your work? Living in the South and being introduced to "keeper" moonshine has greatly affected my life! I'm now one of the only women in America to found and operate a whiskey distillery. The South has totally shaped and enriched my life.

Do you have a daily routine? Every day for me is a new day. I have to change hats continuously in order to run my business well. Mostly I try my best to stay in touch with the amazing people I meet in the marketplace. They are the folks who help our brands grow and flourish.

What was the moment you decided to start making moonshine? The minute I tasted "keeper" moonshine, the kind that never leaves the home place. I knew I had to learn how to make this amazing, totally American product, and bring it to the market.

Where did you learn your craft? I studied with mountain moonshine makers and then broadened my search to the Southern states. I also took master distilling classes with my husband, Charlie, and we perfected our craft by trial and error. Today, we consult with some of the country's finest master distillers to be sure we stay on top of our game.

Flying Cloud Farm

who — **Annie Louise Perkinson**
Isaiah Perkinson
location — **Fairview, North Carolina**

Flying Cloud Farm is located about twelve miles southeast of Asheville in a valley in the town of Fairview. For nearly twelve years, Annie Louise Perkinson and her husband, Isaiah, have been farming on the fourteen acres of rich bottomland, following organic methods. They produce vegetables, fruits, and flowers for local markets, and they sell straight to their customers through a one-hundred-member CSA; at farmers' markets; and through their honor-system self-service roadside stand. They strongly believe in selling only what they grow, and working directly with the people who are eating their food.

Annie Louise comes from a family of farmers. Her cousins run Hickory Nut Gap Farm, a nearby sustainable meat operation. Although she did not grow up wanting to be a farmer, after spending time on organic farms in Germany and England in her twenties, she decided she wanted to continue her work on her family's land in North Carolina. When she met Isaiah, they succeeded in making this dream a reality. They now work and live on the farm, raising their two daughters, Sidney Rose and Ivy, along with their five dogs: Okra, Poppy, Rocket (a type of arugula), Sparkles, and Massey (a new puppy named by Ivy and Isaiah after the family tractor, a Massey Ferguson).

Annie Louise, Isaiah, and the Flying Cloud crew grow and harvest vegetables, fruits, and flowers on their fourteen-acre farm in Fairview. Their self-service stand, on the edge of the property, is filled with seasonal delights— cosmos, zinnias, dahlias, and fresh produce.

What do you enjoy most about living on a farm? Walking to work, picking flowers, working with my husband, waking up to the birds chirping outside my window, having my kids close by, working with awesome food.

Do you have a daily routine? We wake up at 6 am, work hard all day long, and go to bed by 10 pm. The eight hours of sleep are essential to restore from the physical work. On weekdays I get the kids ready for school, pack lunches, make a picking list, then go to work by 7:30 or 8 am. The days vary. Sometimes we are harvesting, washing, and packing produce. Other days we are picking flowers and making bouquets. Other days we are hoeing, digging potatoes, or starting seeds. It is a seasonal life that changes with the weather all along the way. We have to be willing to be flexible.

Describe the farm. We grow on fourteen acres of wonderful bottomland in Fairview, following organic methods. Our produce is sold directly to our consumers through our CSA, at farmers' markets, and through our roadside stand. We firmly believe in working directly with the people who are eating our food, and being straightforward and honest. Our primary crops are vegetables of many varieties, flowers throughout the season, and blueberries, strawberries, and blackberries. Isaiah and I work together with a crew of people to grow the food and get it out of our fields and onto the plates of our community.

What is your favorite flower? Right now it's dahlias, because that is what's blooming. I truly fall in love with whatever is in season. Lately I keep finding myself patting and rubbing the winter squashes, almost as if they were children. They are so cute, and it is a bit of an ordeal to get them raised after all.

All questions answered by Annie Louise Perkinson

SOUTH CAROLINA

Tucked into South Carolina's picturesque coastline, where the Ashley and Cooper Rivers meet, Charleston is the state's oldest city. History is evident everywhere in its perfectly preserved buildings and beautiful landscapes. This charming Southern locale is known for its hot, humid climate, moss-covered trees, and wholehearted hospitality. In the 1920s, the Charleston Renaissance movement embraced artists, jazz musicians, and such innovations as the cocktail party and the Charleston dance craze; today these influences are still felt in the works of makers Magar Hatworks and Jack Rudy Cocktail Co. The city's long traditions of craftsmanship and storytelling—not to mention art, design, and food—are celebrated in the rich and varied works of Sweeteeth, Sisal and Tow, Moran Woodworked Furniture, Finkelstein's Center, Proud Mary, and Middleton Made Knives.

Sweeteeth

who — **Johnny Battles**
location — **North Charleston, South Carolina**

Chocolatier Johnny Battles describes Sweeteeth as "handcrafted chocolatey goodness with a twist." The twist is the unique, inspired flavor combinations of his chocolate bars and bonbons, from mainstays such as peanut butter and chipotle, ginger and popping sugar, and port wine caramel to seasonal offerings such as ruby red grapefruit and basil, jalapeno and pineapple, and more.

Johnny is as fun and energetic as the candy he makes. A true Southerner, originally from Alabama, he has lived in Charleston since 2002. He began experimenting with chocolate while working at EVO Pizzeria in North Charleston. His truffles made it to the dessert menu, and word spread fast. Soon, other Charleston shops began asking for Johnny's chocolates. In 2008, when he found out he was going to be a father, he decided to branch out and start his chocolate and sweet business, Sweeteeth.

Johnny uses single-origin Colombian chocolate for all his treats, carefully crafting each bar or bonbon through small-batch production. A self-professed flavor maker, Johnny's innovative pairings are shaped by his ideas regarding Southern life and enjoyment, particularly notes that remind him of his childhood. "Nothing fancy," he explains. "You can just effortlessly enjoy certain things, and those are the bites I like best." Johnny's "crazy addictive" fillings, as he calls them, are today satisfying sweet teeth across the country.

From his chocolate factory
in North Charleston, Johnny
handcrafts each bar and bonbon,
filling the molds with creative
concoctions such as peanut
butter and chipotle, then hand-
wrapping the treats with
his sweet, colorful designs.

How has living in the South influenced your work? The general personality that comes from each bar is about both flavor and indulgence. How we enjoy things in the South.

Did you have another career before starting Sweeteeth? I've spent 90 percent of my working life in some type of kitchen setting. Kitchen life wasn't always seen as cool and desirable to the general public. It's hard and not always rewarding, especially for a twenty-year-old line cook. But with time it can get real, real sweet.

What was the moment you decided to start your business? The starting of the business was a progression, but the actual step to create it and attempt to live from it started when I realized I was going to be a dad. I wanted to create a different kind of example and I could schedule my time to better suit the demands of the little one.

Where does your business name come from? Lauren, my wife, came up with it as a play on a mouthful of sweet teeth. We used to call it Johnny's Sweeteeth and just shortened it to better

separate it from my personal identity. Like my son, I want my business to grow up to be better than me!

Why chocolate? The thing I liked about baking was the demand for precision and the constant threat of failure if steps were missed or neglected. That is even more the case with chocolate and sugar. I was working with it just to see how far it could go and what tricks you could play with it as a medium. It was more fun and far more exciting than I'd expected, and now it's five years later.

What is the best part of working with your hands? It just feels good when you can relate in some small way to each little step. I have a hand in the making, filling, capping, wrapping, and shipping of each chocolate bar or bonbon that leaves the shop. They're my little buddies and I love them all because I make them all.

What is your future plan for Sweeteeth? I like to imagine a life in the mountains or in a magical forest with a Hansel and Gretel candy kitchen where I can make chocolate all day and make fires with Liam all night—and have internet.

106

-UPC to
-CARAMEL
+Both
-PB+C
Full
-Ship
-Bank
-Paypal
+Aspen
Stella Nuva
Aspen
Call
Ginn
PB+C
ACH

Magar Hatworks

who — **Leigh Magar**
location — **Charleston, South Carolina**

Designer Leigh Magar has one foot in the past and one firmly in the present. Using centuries-old techniques, she custom-makes hats for modern men and women. Her studio, Magar Hatworks, is located in a charming nineteenth-century house in a residential neighborhood of Charleston. Here, she hosts seasonal tea parties, where guests show off their hats in true Southern style.

Leigh grew up in the mill town of Spartanburg, South Carolina. She was a sculptor, first making crowns out of found objects, velvet, wire, and beads, then became enamored with functional headwear. She studied millinery at the Fashion Institute of Technology (FIT) in New York while working as a live-in maid. During school, she assisted the famous milliner Rod Keenan in his Harlem studio.

After returning to the South, she got a wholesale order from Barneys New York, and has been making hats ever since.

When Leigh took her first millinery class at FIT, she fell in love with the gorgeous antique wooden forms used to shape hats. They spoke to her sculptor roots. Forms have been used since the fifteenth century; hat makers manipulate material over the form, then use steam to mold it into shape. Leigh began collecting vintage forms from flea markets, and after a generous donation from a collector she now has almost four hundred in her "hat block museum."

On a recent trip to Paris, Leigh came up with the idea for a new label, Madame Magar. This expanded collection includes dresses and accessories, all made by hand.

Leigh's millinery straddles the worlds of centuries-old trade and modern accessory design. Her colorful, inspiration-filled studio and shop is also home to her hat block museum. The antique wooden forms take up an entire wall of her quintessentially charming Charleston house.

110

What brought you to Charleston?
The sea and the famous flapper dance, the Charleston—it was born here!

How has living in the South influenced your work? As a girl, growing up in a small mill town, I dreamed of living in New York and did not appreciate the small wonders of the South: pimento cheese, sweet tea. I followed my dream by attending the Fashion Institute of Technology for millinery. The city was so inspiring with its jewels: museums, supply shops, films, music, and ethnic food. Yet I longed for the slower-paced, soothing South, where I now have a circa-1825 studio/shop with a large porch for seasonal tea parties and a garden with pomegranate and fig trees.

Describe your new Madame Magar line. For Madame Magar, I create things that I love, beyond my hats. The line includes sculpture, dresses, dolls, accessories, and more, all made by hand in my studio. The first collection was influenced by my grandmother and her sisters, who were quilters, farmers, cooks, seamstresses, storytellers. The graceful slowness of the South has always been inherent in my work; it's what has set me apart. My grandmother's Sunday dinners, her garden existence, celebrating the old ways by canning vegetables from her garden and living simply. These cherished crafts are the heart of Madame Magar.

Where do you source the materials used in your work? I have collected vintage materials since high school. My town had amazing thrift stores, where my friends and I would fight with old women over leopard coats. Madame Magar uses local fabrics as much as possible. This is especially important to me since my hometown has been so hurt by factory closings. I use a lot of fabric from Read Brothers, a time capsule of a store in Charleston since 1912.

What is the best part of working with your hands? "An artist is never poor." That is from the film *Babette's Feast*. I can't imagine not creating objects. It's great to make things that you desire. It's like magic, Madame Magar!

111

Sisal and Tow

who — **Becca Barnet**
location — **Charleston, South Carolina**

Becca Barnet's apartment in Charleston's Harleston Village resembles a cabinet of curiosities. You might see just about anything here: taxidermy, models, mounts, sculptural pieces. (Her bull terrier, Bruce, seems to take it all in stride.) The apartment serves as Becca's fabrication studio, where, as she says, she'll make *anything* by hand.

Becca grew up in nearby Spartanburg, South Carolina. She recalls being intrigued by sculpture and fabrication as a child; on trips to Walt Disney World she would wonder who made the amazing three-dimensional backdrops. She studied illustration at the Rhode Island School of Design and spent six weeks in an intensive certification program at the Missouri Taxidermy Institute. After graduating in 2009 she took an internship at the American Museum of Natural History. The museum soon hired her full time, and she gained experience learning the tricks of the trade of re-creating nature in various materials.

In Charleston she found the space she needed to create her own works—interesting one-offs that honor and celebrate nature. Each is unique and fits perfectly in the space for which it is made. Her goals for Sisal and Tow include gallery, studio, and education elements. But, most of all, she'd just like it to be known as a company that makes really special things.

From bobby pins to snakeskins, Becca's fabrication studio contains all the tools, supplies, and curiosities necessary for her meticulous nature re-creations. Through taxidermy and other modeling techniques, she gives new life to creatures great and small.

How has living in the South influenced your work? Growing up in the South introduced me to a rich culture built on hard work, hand-crafted objects, folk art, and storytelling.

Where does your business name come from? It is named as such for two reasons: First, my great-great grandfather began a textile business in the late 1800s that my father later owned and operated until the early 2000s. Secondly, sisal and tow are both twines used frequently in the earliest and most archaic forms of taxidermy. Basically, they are what the inventors of taxidermy used to form the musculature of their mounts.

What was the moment you decided to start your business? My father asked me what my life goal was, and I blurted out something to the extent of "to own a fabrication business, where I can make anything for anyone, from museum exhibits to personal artifact mounts. To have my own studio." He told me I had his support. I realized it didn't have to be just a dream.

What is the best part of working with your hands? That completely exhilarating feeling I get when I'm sculpting. And going from sweaty and frustrated to really pleasantly surprised and sometimes completely amazed that what I did actually worked.

What objects do you most enjoy making? I most enjoy sculpting to re-create natural textures. For example, taking a piece of wood and adding (false) branches to it; if I can make it look like it is a real piece of wood with no alteration, I've succeeded. The cool part is what I can make the false branches do or "say."

Describe some of the tools you use in your work. I always have my drill, Dremel, and small sculpting tools with me. I use a lot of sand-paper, and popsicle sticks for mixing. I never know when I will need my heat gun or something inventive for texture, like tinfoil, sponges, or mesh.

Do you have a dream project? I have so many dream projects. I'd love to restore a series of old dioramas. I'd love to make a diorama! I'd love to repair a large taxidermy collection from the 1940s. I'd love to make a giant interactive installation of a honeycomb so that children could learn about bees. I'd be happy with just about any project. So, keep them coming.

Moran Woodworked Furniture

who — **Celia Gibson**
Michael James Moran
location — **Charleston, South Carolina**

When you drive up to Michael Moran's workshop in Charleston, you may be greeted first by a friendly greyhound named Addie—soon followed by the equally welcoming Michael and his partner, Celia Gibson. On their blog, they call themselves "arboreal eccentrics." Love of wood shines through in every aspect of their workspace: the wood-drying room Michael built with his own hands, the light-filled workshop, the beautiful office. They grow vegetables in a garden behind the shop.

A native of Kentucky, Michael moved to South Carolina to play soccer for the College of Charleston. After college, he stayed, apprenticing with a furniture maker and woodworker in town, and in 2004 he started Moran Woodworked Furniture. Celia grew up in the Southeast, moving around between Georgia, Alabama, Tennessee, and Virginia. She studied abroad, received a master's degree in literature at University College London, then returned to the South and joined Michael. Since 2010 the couple has lived and worked together, designing and building bespoke furniture and sculpture. They collaborate on the designs, then Michael crafts the pieces while Celia handles sales.

Their furniture is classic in form and function—tables, benches, cabinets, and other household pieces—yet each work represents their distinctive, contemporary point of view. Their goal is to honor the natural beauty of wood through traditional craftsmanship, the responsible selection of materials, and a modern approach to design.

Celia and Michael's well-kept workshop is a showcase for the couple's favorite resource, trees. From the elegant Window Table to the Long, Long Bench, each Moran Woodworked piece celebrates the natural beauty of the material. In the yard, Addie, the greyhound, protects the drying planks.

How did you become interested in woodworking? *Michael:* I grew up around the notion that if you needed something, you figured out how to build it. My older sister, a metal sculptor for many years, helped to cultivate my interests and perspectives on art early in life. I've always had a great love of trees, and when I met the furniture maker I later worked for, it all fell into place.

What was the moment you decided to start your business? *Michael:* I had been apprenticing as a woodworker and furniture maker for three years. Working under a craftsman taught me more than just a skill; it helped me uncover my own priorities and proclivities. Eventually it came time for me to make my own work. I had a lot of energy, a strong notion of what I wanted to do, and no money or business knowledge. So, I guess you could say the conditions were perfect.

What is your favorite product? *Celia:* Every piece has its own quiddity, but for me building a dining table is my favorite. A table is a piece of furniture for loved ones to gather around to eat and drink, laugh and cry. It holds an intimacy that few other objects can maintain.

Michael: And every tabletop is a large, uninterrupted expanse of wood grain, the beautiful documentation of a tree's history. It represents a unique opportunity to herald the beauty of wood.

What is the most satisfying part of your making process? *Michael:* There is a spark that happens when you are in the midst of building a piece: sometimes a giant "aha," sometimes a small nod. It seems to be when you start to understand something about what you are working with, and what might be the best way to translate this beautiful piece of wood into a piece of furniture.

Where do you source your materials? *Celia:* We work only with "good wood," whose origins we know. Whether it is reclaimed from storm-downed trees or family-run mills, we support the practices we believe in: responsible stewardship, ecological soundness, locality, and respect and understanding regarding materials.

Finkelstein's Center

who — **Michelle Jewell**
location — **Charleston, South Carolina**

With the flip of a coin, Michelle Jewell and her husband decided to move to Charleston. Three years later, in early 2010, she started Finkelstein's Center, a toy workshop. (Her dog, Bernard Pickles Finkelstein Jewell Amick, aka Bernie, is the company's namesake.) Michelle creates an eclectic mix of plush toy characters inspired by creatures great and small, real and imagined.

"Blimey! It's handmade," reads the sign that welcomes visitors to Finkelstein's lofty studio in downtown Charleston. And it's true: Michelle constructs each animal, monster, or other critter by hand. Her organic toy-making process begins with an illustration that offers the first glimpse of the toy's personality. Without a pattern, she hand cuts the pieces, then sews, stuffs,

and accessorizes the character, upcycling old sweaters, shirts, and other fabrics into clothing, making beards out of buttons, and so on. Each irresistible piece is one of a kind—from Maude the Lamb to Glasses Kitty to Stick Friends (a collection of animated sticks) to Barnum (a giant octopus created for Spoleto, the city's annual performing arts festival). Next up, as nominated by her customers, the lovable, slow-moving Sloth.

Michelle's cuddly menagerie has been featured in local exhibitions and can be found in stores around the country. Through her "custom animals, commissioned creatures, and other odd ideas," as she calls them, Michelle's Finkelstein's Center has become a successful, and much-beloved, center for creativity.

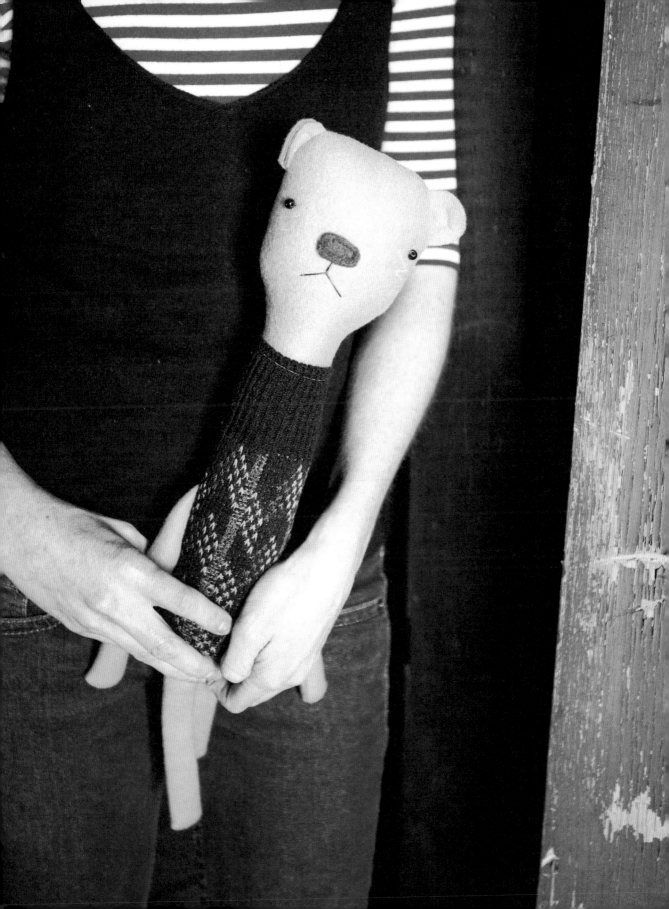

Each of Michelle's charmingly quirky characters receives the utmost attention to detail, from the first sketch to the final stitch. Her lofty Charleston studio contains cabinets (and suitcases) stuffed with mermaids, hound dogs, and other lovable creatures.

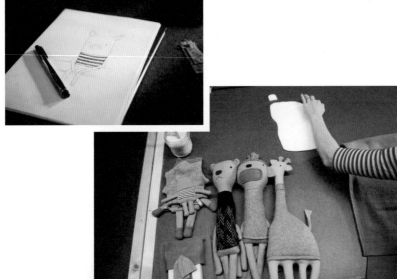

Learning any trade is rewarding, especially when you look back and see how you've improved. It encourages me to try new things that might have intimidated me before.

Describe your studio. My studio is in a warehouse on upper Meeting Street, in downtown Charleston. I share a space with the Rewined Candle factory. It has old wooden floors, cinderblock walls, and lofty ceilings with rafters full of ancient-looking conveyors. It was stark, so we built storage closets with colorful reclaimed doors and huge rolling workbenches that are pretty handy for fabricating large-scale creatures. We've got card catalogs and huge chalkboards to help me stay organized. Across the hall is a rooftop garden that overlooks Meeting Street and the Ravenel Bridge.

Describe a bit about what you do. I create characters through illustration, then I build them into fabric sculptures with free-hand cutting and sewing. I also do gallery pieces and commissioned works. These range from family and wedding dolls to custom creatures and large-scale pieces. And I collaborate with other artists to turn their two-dimensional characters into three dimensions.

What is the most satisfying part of your making process? I like that moment of anticipation between sewing and stuffing. The pieces are stitched inside out, and when I flip a sewn piece, I get the first glimpse of where the character's personality is headed.

What characters do you most enjoy making? Woodland animals in well-tailored clothes, creatures of folklore, mythical sea monsters, tradesmen, animal-human hybrids, characters with medical oddities.

What has been your favorite project? I had the opportunity to build a giant octopus for a Spoleto event last year. He had twelve-foot bendable tentacles that were covered with five hundred hand-stitched buttons for suckers. I also worked on a sailor series that involved hand-stitched button beards and hand-embroidered tattoos. I enjoy the meticulous, attention-to-detail projects the best.

Where did you learn your craft? My mother taught me to sew when I was young; she was a talented seamstress. Learning to develop and build characters, on the other hand, involved a lot of trial and error.

What is the best part of working with your hands? It's cathartic. For some reason, my brain gets quiet when my hands are busy. Learning any trade is rewarding, especially when you get a chance to look back and see how you've improved. It encourages me to try new things that might have intimidated me before.

Jack Rudy Cocktail Co.

who — **Brooks Reitz**
location — **Charleston, South Carolina**

Jack Rudy was "a curious type who made his own bullets, and shot them into a dirt wall he constructed in his basement. In addition to being a 'marvelous' dancer, he loved to entertain and was known to overindulge in drink, smoke, and his wife's gourmet cooking." This memorable biographical sketch features prominently on the label of the company's signature product, its Small Batch Tonic. Founder Brooks Reitz named the business after his great-grandfather, whom he never met but heard remarkable stories about during his youth in Henderson, Kentucky.

Brooks was working as the general manager of FIG, a Charleston favorite, when he began making his own tonic to supplement his bar repertoire. He created a syrup made of quinine, a delicate mix of botanicals, and real cane sugar that happens to be a perfect complement to gin. He put it on the menu at FIG. And that's how Jack Rudy got its start.

With favorable press coverage, Jack Rudy grew quickly. Brooks is now the general manager of The Ordinary, a new seafood restaurant, and runs Jack Rudy (with help from his cousin) on the side. Brooks credits the food culture in the South for shaping his career. Like the establishments where he's worked, he believes in using only the best ingredients. For his newest product, Small Batch Grenadine, he sources fresh pomegranate juice from a family farm in California. For Jack Rudy, the goal is to continue to identify overlooked staples of the classic American bar, make them new, and develop customer relationships that last a lifetime.

Batch Nº

000043

JACK RUDY COCKTAIL CO.

SMALL BATCH TONIC

Handcrafted in the South

17 *fl oz*
503 *ml*

From his Charleston house—the Jack Rudy Cocktail Co. headquarters—Brooks processes a batch of his new grenadine with fresh pomegranate juice and prepares to pack and ship his signature tonic.

What do you enjoy most about living in Charleston? The weather (nearly always sunny), the vibrant food community, the youth (there are several colleges in town), the activity (paddleboarding, kayaking, biking, running, surfing), and the history. It's hard to pinpoint just one element, but Charleston is among the most beautiful cities in America.

How has the South influenced your work? Everything I've done for my job, and in particular Jack Rudy Cocktail Co., has been filtered through a Southern lens, which means it's been informed deeply by the history of the South.

What is the most satisfying part of your making process? When a customer reaches out to tell me how much they enjoy what I've done. When I'm surrounded by tonic all day—producing, packing, shipping—it's easy to get a little disconnected, but when I find that it's introduced some little piece of enjoyment to someone's day, that's pretty awesome.

What first sparked your interest in working in the spirit/beverage industry? Growing up in Kentucky with bourbon in my backyard certainly made that interest innate. After graduating from college, I went to work at a restaurant with an incredible bar—stocked with what might have been one of the most varied liquor selections in the country. All that stuff at my fingertips made me very excited about all the things I still had to learn.

Where did you learn your craft? I learned how to bartend from an old, surly bartender in Lexington, Kentucky, and then I really honed the craft of creating when I moved to Louisville and was charged with making a beverage program, more or less out of thin air.

What are your influences? I can usually trace every element of something I've created to a memory, a person, or an interaction. It's so important to expose yourself to all kinds of people and experiences, as it makes us so much richer as makers and entrepreneurs.

Proud Mary

who — **Harper Poe**
location — **Charleston, South Carolina**

A native of Charlotte, North Carolina, Harper Poe led a peripatetic existence after college, spending time in Costa Rica, France, Colorado, Los Angeles, and New York before returning to the South. Eventually she settled in the historic city of Charleston. Her business, Proud Mary, reflects her international outlook and her dual passion for handcrafted textiles and contemporary design. Harper designs the items, including housewares, shoes, and accessories, and artisans in Mali, Peru, Morocco, and Guatemala make them using traditional methods.

This is sustainable design; fair trade is as important as color, pattern, and material.

"Pride not pity" is Harper's straightforward motto. The goods are a celebration of the people and cultures that create them, she says.

Harper's goals for Proud Mary include reaching out to artisans in other countries with strong textile traditions, such as the Philippines, Ethiopia, Cambodia, and Vietnam. She imagines expanding her rug offerings and collection of wearables. Eventually she'd like to start a distribution company to sell the goods of artisans who are making beautiful products—not necessarily textiles—that are underrepresented in the marketplace. And to this well-traveled, globally minded entrepreneur, Charleston's creative community feels like home.

Harper's bright studio features an inspiring mix of colors, textures, and cultures from around world, which is reflected in the rich, bold designs of Proud Mary's home and clothing offerings.

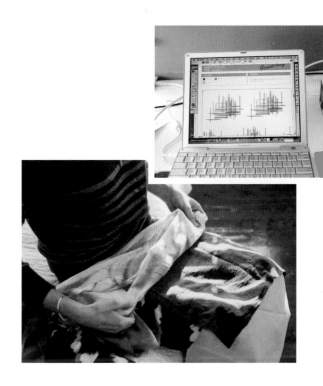

How has living in the South influenced your work? Partly in a practical sense, in that the lower cost of living has allowed me to put more time and energy into Proud Mary—which has paid off. Charleston has a wonderful entrepreneurial spirit; there is a large and inspiring community of small business owners. Creatively, the South has a great textile and craft tradition, especially indigo and sweet grass baskets originating from West Africa. I recently started working in West Africa and love feeling the connection between the crafts surrounding me in Charleston and those in Africa.

What was the moment you decided to start your business? After returning from volunteering with Habitat for Humanity in South America. I had fallen in love with traditional textiles and wanted to figure out a way to combine that with my love for contemporary textiles and design while giving back to artisan communities.

What is the best part of working with artisans? Getting to know them. I feel so lucky to be able to have relationships with people all over the world who are so different from me but at the end of the day want the same things: to be able to support themselves, spend time with loved ones, and laugh.

Did you have another career before starting Proud Mary? I had a million jobs before Proud Mary: waitress, wedding planner, project manager for a construction company, interior design assistant. I was never good at working for someone else.

What are your influences? Travel, *The Alchemist*, the blog *A Gypsea Dreamer*, Sonia Delaunay textiles, the Southwest, Georgia O'Keeffe, vintage textiles, Japanese *shibori* and *boro*, indigenous costumes, and contemporary fashion.

Middleton Made Knives

who — **Quintin Middleton**
location — **Saint Stephen, South Carolina**

Quintin Middleton's workshop is located in the rural town of Saint Stephen, approximately fifty miles north of historic Charleston. Tucked behind his house, the small, humble shed (constructed of two-by-fours and plywood) is home to Middleton Made Knives. Here, he crafts his beautiful and much-celebrated blades, from the classic chef's knife to the paring knife, slicer, shucker, and more.

A self-described "country boy who makes knives," Quintin grew up in nearby Alvin, South Carolina. As a child he was fascinated by heroic characters such as Conan the Barbarian. Setting off on his own adventures, he once tried to make a sword from the metal of an old swing set. This crude attempt got him hooked, and he has been making knives in some form ever since.

Mentored by fellow South Carolina bladesmith Jason Knight, in 2003 Quintin began producing knives professionally (he launched Middleton Made Knives in 2010). His knives are forged in the Damascus tradition, a technique used in swordmaking as early as 300 BC. Using the highest quality materials— from high-carbon steel for his blades to cherry for the handles—Quintin custom shapes each knife with precision and pride. These functional works of art can be found in the kitchens of celebrity chefs and home cooks across the country. Each one is forged in Quintin's tiny, rustic shop.

With humble means—
including a simple backyard
shed and only the essential
tools—Quintin forges custom
knives for celebrated chefs.

146

How has living in the South influenced your work? Charleston has a lot of great chefs—and I want all of them to use my knives.

Do you have a daily routine? My routine is get up around 7 am, kiss my wife and kids, check emails, and go into my shop until 7 pm or later. Then spend the rest of the evening with my family.

What was the moment you decided to start your business? When I didn't want to work on anything but knives.

How did you become interested in knife making? From watching movies in which a hero forges a sword and heads off on an adventure.

Where did you learn your craft? I was pointed in the right direction by my mentor, Jason Knight, a master bladesmith. The rest is by trail and error and talent from God.

What is the most satisfying part of your making process? The finished product is the most satisfying. Making something from nothing but hard work (and an achy body) is very satisfying.

What tools and materials do you use to make your knives? Belt grinders, drill presses, a kiln, glue, steel, and wood.

What is the best part of working with your hands? Work is like meditation for me. It gives me time to pray and talk to Jesus.

Whom have you been most excited to make a knife for? Chefs Emeril Lagasse, Robert Irvine, Guy Fieri, Michael Chiarello, and Michael Rhulman.

GEORGIA

Athens, Georgia, is situated below the Blue Ridge Mountains, seventy miles northeast of the state's capital, Atlanta. It is a historically creative city that perfectly combines the old and the new. It is home to the University of Georgia (where Megan Fowler of Brown Parcel Press first acquired her printing skills) and filled with antebellum architecture, contemporary art, and diverse nightlife. As one of the South's most progressive culinary scenes, it is ideal for Full Moon Cooperative's produce partnerships with local restaurants. The city also attracts indie music fans from all over the country (it spawned R.E.M. and the B-52s). Its creative and cultural milieu drew photographer Rinne Allen back to her hometown, allowed ceramicist Rebecca Wood to call it home for more than twenty years, and convinced textile designer Susan Hable Smith (of Hable Construction) to move here from New York City.

Full Moon Cooperative

who — **Iwalani Farfour**
Jason Mann
location — **Winterville, Georgia**

Former Californian Jason Mann wears many hats: biodynamic farmer, social and environmental entrepreneur, restaurateur, agro-ecological researcher, and community organizer. He is the founder of Full Moon Cooperative, which began in 2002 as a collective of sustainable fruit and vegetable farms. He started the co-op along with a group of farmers, ecologists, chefs, and educators in Athens, with the mission "to offer innovative farm-based solutions to social, environmental, and economic challenges." They work in partnership with Moonshine Meats (also founded by Jason) to cultivate food throughout the Southeast.

Currently, Full Moon is operating as a small, independent farm. They sell their produce to local restaurants, and to the public through Athens Locally Grown (an online market), the Athens farmers' market, and their CSA. Full Moon works in collaboration with their sister company, Farm 255, a celebrated farm-to-table restaurant located downtown. Farm manager Iwalani Farfour and award-winning chef Whitney Otawka coordinate on the farm's crop plan, ensuring a kitchen stocked with local, seasonal produce and a daily menu filled with fresh, flavorful Southern simplicity. The goal of the co-op and restaurant is to make everyday "good food"— food that is locally sourced, seasonal, steeped in tradition and narrative, and able to connect people to each other and to their community.

Located on the outskirts of
Athens, the small but diverse
Full Moon Farm provides
fresh produce to local favorite
Farm 255 (and the on-the-go
Farm Cart).

What do you enjoy most about working on a farm? I love watching a tiny seed grow into an edible, beautiful vegetable. I love being outdoors and being a part of the ever-changing landscape, noticing the light and the wind and the soil, how they are never the same and how each one affects the other. I love that I have tangible customers, and that I can see the smiles on their faces and the joy in their hearts from eating something I have grown.

Describe the farm. In the past, we have participated in a cooperative—two to three farms sharing produce. At the moment, we are operating one farm. It is very small, a little over one acre, and diversified. We are closely associated with a restaurant downtown called Farm 255, with a vision of farm-to-table. We work with the head chef, Whitney Otawka, to build our crop plan so as to keep her kitchens stocked with local, seasonal produce. We also run a CSA with close to seventy members. We do all of this with one full-time manager, two part-time employees, and myself.

What is the most satisfying part of physical farm work? Physical activity makes me happy and balanced. No matter how exhausted I am at the end of the day, I am always grateful to be healthy and strong and to know that with my own two hands I have moved the earth and created something beautiful.

Do you have a favorite growing season? Spring. It is a new beginning and everything is full of possibilities. Throughout the winter we work on our crop plan, and it finally gets implemented in spring. All your hard work is laid out in front of you, and it is wonderful. The weather is perfect and the weeds and the insects have yet to set in.

How do you think the farm has influenced the community? I hope we have shown others that they can have a say in how they live their lives. We can help them achieve a healthy diet, support their local economy, and learn about their food. We have also supported farmers in our community to grow bigger and better sustainably.

All questions answered by Iwalani Farfour

Hable Construction

who — **Susan Hable Smith**
location — **Athens, Georgia**

Painter and textile designer Susan Hable Smith is a ball of creative energy. Her Victorian home in Athens exudes playfulness in the art, textiles, and colors that Susan surrounds herself with. For Hable Construction—a company Susan formed with her sister, Katharine Hable Sweeney—Susan turns her own colorful paintings into repeatable surface patterns for use on products such as furniture, pillows, and totes.

A Texas native, Susan lived in New York City for twelve years. She and her husband fell in love with Athens on a weekend trip to visit her friend, the photographer Rinne Allen. They weren't sure they were ready to leave New York, but they knew Athens would be the perfect place to raise their two young children, Lake and Bird.

As it turns out, Athens has given her the space she needed; she has met like-minded people and become involved in the creative community here in this university town. Relocating to Georgia also enabled her to expand her business by putting her closer to North Carolina's furniture and textile mills. She now works in a separate studio just a stone's throw away from the back door of her house.

Although they no longer live in the same city, Susan and her sister still work together daily—Katharine on sales, Susan on creative work. For Hable Construction, integrity, freedom, and flexibility are imperative. Susan takes pride in working with factories in the United States whenever she can, collaborating with people she genuinely enjoys, and staying as creative as possible while having fun.

Susan's love of color shows
in the spectrum of her patterns
and the vibrant collections
that fill her whitewashed
workspace—a circa 1918
mill village house that was
carefully deconstructed,
moved, and reconstructed
on Susan's property.

What do you enjoy most about living in Athens? I absolutely love the diversity of people who live here. The University of Georgia brings so many different talents to Athens, and I try to keep myself involved in the textile program there. Many of my friends choose to live in Athens but work in New York, London, Los Angeles, Copenhagen, etc., so someone is always traveling and returning with great stories and inspiration.

How does the South influence your work? I was fearful of leaving the energy of a very active studio in New York, but being back here has surprised me in a good way. I have more space to think and make and do. I have found time to paint, which has added a wonderful element to my work. I have met people and worked on projects in the Southeast thanks to my close proximity to North Carolina and the furniture and textile mills. I have opened my eyes to many other facets of the textile industry. I've mentored students in the textile program at the university. All of this is a different but great energy that I didn't know existed until moving here.

Describe your studio. We deconstructed and moved a circa 1918 mill village house from a town fifty miles down the road to my backyard. We put it back together, using every bit of wood from its original structure, and gave it a new roof. We vaulted the ceilings and whitewashed the entire interior surface. We added an enclosed kitchen on the back that was originally a screened porch. All of the floors are original. While working on the house, we found all kinds of objects in the walls: a skeleton key, baby shoe, corncob pipe, spoon, magnet, and child's top. Amazing!

What is the most satisfying part of your making process? I love it when I randomly pick up my paintbrush and make a pattern that is sensible, graphic, and happy all at once. I love when my art inspires a person to smile and tell me about it. Mostly, I find that if I please myself, then I can please someone else with what I make.

Do you have a dream project you would like to work on? I'm always looking ahead and dreaming of something bigger. I think that's why I'm never bored—I have way too many things to do in this lifetime!

Brown Parcel Press

who — **Megan Fowler**
location — **Sparta, Georgia**

Megan Fowler and her husband, Brad, live with their young daughter Emolyn on the thirty-one-acre Three Centuries Farm in Sparta, Georgia. When not running her letterpress business, Megan works with her husband raising livestock on their land, producing heritage-breed pork and free-range eggs.

Brown Parcel Press is run out of a 1920s-era former general store located on their property. The charming building sits across from their home, complete with floor-to-ceiling wooden shelves, a porch, and an out-of-use gas pump. Creating within a building filled with rich history inspires Megan's work and work ethic immensely. Her spacious studio more than accommodates her large, heavy equipment, including two vintage letterpresses—a Heidelberg Windmill and a Vandercook SP-20—and an antique paper cutter. Megan loves living a little off the beaten path in rural Sparta. It feels like home and she thrives on the sense of community that surrounds her.

Megan took her first letterpress class at the University of Georgia. She is drawn to the beautiful impressions, the crispness and clarity of the print. She also appreciates the physicality of the work, and feeling a connection to each piece that runs through the press. Her prints reflect her daily life, incorporating nature, animals, fruits and vegetables—often inspired by what is in season on her farm—and traditional Southern foods. She loves the sense of having accomplished something at the end of the day, starting with blank pieces of paper and ending with a stack of colorful prints—and ink-smudged hands.

Megan's Heidelberg Windmill and Vandercook SP-20 letterpresses occupy center stage in the converted 1920s general store. Her crisp, colorful prints reflect her daily life on the farm—inspired by animals, fruits, vegetables, and more.

Some people are beach people, some are mountain people, some are city people, and some are just Southern people.

How has living in the South influenced your work? I think it's only human to be influenced by your surroundings, which is why it's so important to put yourself in an environment that affects you positively. Some people are beach people, some are mountain people, some are city people, and some are just Southern people.

Describe your studio. I work in a 1920s general store that is now on my family's farm. It used to be the place to get cheese, gas, penny candy, and even your mail. It is this building that cemented my love affair with this place. It inspires my work and work ethic immensely.

Where does your business name come from? I love packaging. I almost feel like the presentation of a gift or package is more important than the gift itself. Almost. I want my work to give that feeling of receiving something beautiful and simple.

What is the most satisfying part of your making process? I love pulling the first print of a project. My prints start from pencil drawings before going to the computer and finally the press. The color and impression on a clean sheet of paper—I'm always surprised to see how well it comes together!

Do you have a daily routine? Yes, being a farmer, a printer, and a mom means a lot of the success of my day depends on routine. There are daily farm chores, which have to get done morning and evening, and printing and "momming" fills out the rest of it.

How has having a baby changed your business or creative process? It has made me a lot more focused. Because I don't have a guaranteed eight consecutive hours of work time each day, I have to really focus on the task at hand. When I'm spending time with my daughter, I want to use my energy for and put all my attention on her. And the same goes for printing. I have such a newfound respect for moms.

What are your influences? The natural world, Roald Dahl, the Breton flag, cotton, saffron threads, linen, alliteration, my family.

Rinne Allen Photographs

who — **Rinne Allen**
location — **Athens, Georgia**

Rinne Allen was born and raised in Athens. After attending art school in Tennessee and living in Paris for a short time, she returned to her hometown, which provides a beautiful and artful setting for her work and family life. Rinne is a photographer and spends the majority of her time documenting the process of growing and making things. In each of her photographs, she attempts to show the touch of the hand.

Rinne's studio is located on the edge of downtown in a once-dilapidated, one-hundred-year-old house. With her husband, she reworked and restored the downstairs for her workspace. Keeping much of the original patina and layers of plaster on the walls, they also created a darkroom for photo developing and printing.

The space opens onto a lush garden (with a near year-round growing calendar) that leads to a wooded area near a creek. It is the perfect place to collect specimens for her light drawings. For these drawings, Rinne works with cyanotype and sepia to give a beautiful blue and brown tone to her prints. She mixes her own chemicals in much the same way as it was done in the nineteenth century.

Rinne is a consummate maker. In addition to her photography, she has a deep interest in textiles, works in ceramics, makes books, gardens, and creates flower arrangements. Her studio is a magical space, reflecting her creative way of living and filled with interesting collections from her travels and many projects.

In the garden surrounding her studio, Rinne gathers specimens for her ethereal light drawings. Inside, the restored century-old house is filled with Southern charm and collections from her travels.

How has living in the South influenced your work? Being in the South completely influences me. Influences seep into you around here. There are things that I see every day that suddenly will spark an idea, or things that are new and fresh that trigger something else. It could be something I saw on a walk, or in a book, or that a friend made. I spend a lot of time with books, and wandering flea markets, looking for lost things. Weeding in the garden brings on a lot of ideas too.

Describe your light drawings. There is something really freeing and fundamental about light drawings. They are free of technology and machines and involve just the simple principles of light and composition. It's one of the earliest photographic processes. You spread a light-sensitive pigment on a surface (in my case, watercolor paper). Once the pigment is dry, the surface is reactive to light. While the paper is drying, I walk through my garden to select specimens. Then, I take them one by one into the sunshine and place them atop the sensitized paper and wait. The specimen leaves its shadow on the paper. Each one is completely unique; I love how unpredictable they are.

Describe your studio. My studio is in the downstairs of an old house that had been condemned by the city. We reworked the space for my studio in 2007. The interior is filled with props and findings and is rich with layers and patina. The studio overlooks our garden. On one side it is shady and cool with north light; on the other, it faces due south with lots of sunshine and flowers and vegetables growing. I love that my studio is next door to my house and that it is surrounded by our garden; out every window there's something green.

Do you have a dream project you would like to work on? My dream project is to live in my hometown and make great work, so each day I try to make that happen.

R. Wood Studio Ceramics

who — **Rebecca Wood**
location — **Athens, Georgia**

Started by self-taught potter Rebecca Wood in 1991, R. Wood Studio Ceramics has grown into one of the largest pottery studios in America. It is a special place where each piece is still entirely made and painted by hand. The ceramics are renowned for their luscious colors, simple shapes, and reflections of Southern surroundings. The studio produces pottery for everyday use as well as one-of-a-kind pieces that are sought after by collectors. All pieces are made from North Carolina red clay (terracotta) and hand-painted with as many as five coats of glaze.

The studio is located in an old produce warehouse in a residential neighborhood near downtown Athens. The welcoming exterior is brightly painted and surrounded by planters made of repurposed tires. The interior is just as inviting: light-filled, with a high ceiling, and overflowing with pottery in vibrant colors and shapes. A creative soul, Rebecca tries to hire smart, artistic self-starters so that she doesn't have to do much managing. (Having the university close by helps.) R. Wood Studio now includes ten artists.

Rebecca herself lives in an old, converted schoolhouse with a large drawing table in the center of her living space. She does a lot of work from home, inspired by her own ceramics and art made by friends. During the workweek, her daily routine involves coffee first; then she lets her inspiration lead her through the day, which usually allows time for gardening, dreaming, and a three- to four-mile run/walk. She often hosts gatherings for creative women, filled with food, wine, and making.

Each R. Wood Ceramics
piece is handmade and
painted in an old produce
warehouse in Athens.
Much of Rebecca's creative
process also happens at
home—whether drawing
and painting or gathering
inspiration while gardening.

How has living in the South influenced your work? The abundant and varied flora inspire me throughout the year. So much lushness, so many shapes, so many colors. The seasons, the weather, always changing from color scheme to color scheme.

Describe your studio. R. Wood Studio is in an old brick produce warehouse near downtown Athens. We've been here twenty-two years. I work at home, too: gardening, canning, drawing, sewing, photographing, painting, and anything else that strikes me.

What hours do you keep? My mind is always at work, mulling over ideas and fine-tuning them in my head. I'm always looking for inspiration and putting ideas together.

What is the most satisfying part of your making process? Sometimes just having the idea is the most fun part. There's no way to bring to reality all the projects and concepts in my head.

When I do complete something and it turns out really well, it's fun to share it with people.

What is the best part of working with your hands? The immediacy of it. Right now, I can create something beautiful or useful out of nothing. Bringing ideas to reality.

Did you have another career before starting R. Wood Studio? I was a checkout girl at a drugstore, then a busboy at a restaurant. Then I worked at a frame shop and a tailor shop. After that, it was all self-employment.

What other types of making do you do? Cooking, jewelry making, flower arranging, wine making, and didgeridoo playing.

What are your influences? Nature. Cézanne is my inspiration for painting. I love fashion and like to keep abreast. I love homesteading crafts and learning to be self-sufficient. My motto is "intuit and do it." My logical brain doesn't really work. My right brain is in charge at all times.

APPENDIX

Makers Index

pp. 58–63

Another Feather
anotherfeather.com
Asheville, NC

pp. 88–93

Asheville Distilling Company
troyandsons.com
12 Old Charlotte Highway
Asheville, NC

pp. 76–81

Bow + Arrow
etsy.com/shop/
bowandarrowapparel
Asheville, NC

pp. 164–69

Brown Parcel Press
brownparcelpress.com
Sparta, GA

pp. 32–37

Emil Erwin
emilerwin.com
Nashville, TN

pp. 82–87

Farm and Sparrow
farmandsparrow.com
Candler, NC

pp. 126–31

Finkelstein's Center
finkcenter.com
Charleston, SC

pp. 64–69

Fleet Co.
fleetcogoods.com
Asheville, NC

pp. 94–99

Flying Cloud Farm
flyingcloudfarm.net
Fairview, NC

pp. 152–57

Full Moon Cooperative
fullmooncoop.org
Winterville, GA

pp. 158–63

Hable Construction
hableconstruction.com
Athens, GA

pp. 44–49
—
Imogene + Willie
imogeneandwillie.com
2601 12th Avenue South
Nashville, TN

pp. 132–37
—
Jack Rudy Cocktail Co.
jackrudycocktailco.com
Charleston, SC

pp. 38–43
—
Jackalope Brewing Company
jackalopebrew.com
701 8th Avenue, South
Nashville, TN

pp. 108–13
—
Magar Hatworks
magarhatworks.com
Charleston, SC

pp. 70–75
—
Melissa Weiss Pottery
melissaweisspottery.com
Asheville, NC

pp. 144–49
—
Middleton Made Knives
middletonmadeknives.com
Saint Stephen, SC

pp. 120–25
—
Moran Woodworked Furniture
moranwoodworked.com
Charleston, SC

pp. 50–55
—
Olive and Sinclair Chocolate Co.
oliveandsinclair.com
Nashville, TN

pp. 26–31
—
Otis James Nashville
otisjamesnashville.com
Nashville, TN

pp. 138–43
—
Proud Mary
proudmary.org
Charleston, SC

pp. 176–81
—
R. Wood Studio Ceramics
rwoodstudio.com
450 Georgia Drive
Athens, GA

pp. 170–75
—
Rinne Allen Photographs
rinneallen.com
Athens, GA

pp. 114–19
—
Sisal and Tow
beccabar.net
Charleston, SC

pp. 102–7
—
Sweeteeth
sweeteethchocolate.com
North Charleston, SC

Southern Favorites

Nashville
—from—

CARRIE AND MATT EDDMENSON

of Imogene + Willie

Asheville
—from—

HANNAH FERRARA

of Another Feather

Charleston
—from—

BROOKS REITZ

of Jack Rudy Cocktail Co.

Athens
—from—

RINNE ALLEN

of Rinne Allen Photographs

NASHVILLE

RESTAURANTS AND CAFÉS

—

Barista Parlor
baristaparlor.com
519 Gallatin Avenue

Burger Up
burger-up.com
2901 12th Avenue South

City House
cityhousenashville.com
1222 4th Avenue North

Margot Café and Bar
margotcafe.com
1017 Woodland Street

Rolf and Daughters
rolfanddaughters.com
700 Taylor Street

Rotier's
rotiersrestaurant.com
2413 Elliston Place

SHOPS

—

Antique Archaeology
antiquearchaeology.com
1300 Clinton Street

E. T. Burk
etburk.com
300 11th Avenue South

Parnassus Books
parnassusbooks.net
3900 Hillsboro Pike

Wonders on Woodland
1110 Woodland Street

MARKETS

—

12 South Farmers' Market
12southfarmersmarket.com
Sevier Park
3000 Granny White Pike

Nashville Farmers' Market
nashvillefarmersmarket.org
900 Rosa L. Parks Boulevard

Nashville Flea Market
nashvilleexpocenter.org/expo/
fleamarket
Tennessee State Fairgrounds
500 Wedgewood Avenue

The Turnip Truck
theturniptruck.com
970 Woodland Street
321 12th Avenue South

LEISURE

—

Belcourt Theatre
belcourt.org
2102 Belcourt Avenue

Frist Center for the Visual Arts
fristcenter.org
919 Broadway

Radnor Lake
radnorlake.org
1160 Otter Creek Road

Schermerhorn Symphony Center
schermerhorncenter.com
1 Symphony Place

The Station Inn
stationinn.com
402 12th Avenue South

ASHEVILLE

RESTAURANTS, CAFÉS, AND BARS

—

The Admiral
theadmiralnc.com
400 Haywood Road

Chai Pani
chaipani.net
22 Battery Park Avenue

Cucina24
cucina24restaurant.com
24 Wall Street

Cúrate
curatetapasbar.com
11 Biltmore Avenue

High Five Coffee Bar
highfivecoffee.com
190 Broadway Street

The Imperial Life
imperialbarasheville.com
48 College Street

The Local Taco
thelocaltaco.com
68 North Lexington Avenue

MG Road
mgroadlounge.com
19 Wall Street

Wicked Weed Brewing
wickedweedbrewing.com
91 Biltmore Avenue

SHOPS

—

Harvest Records
harvest-records.com
415-B Haywood Road

Oddfellows Antiques
oddfellowsasheville.com
124 Swannanoa River Road

Old North
oldnorthclothing.com
82 North Lexington Avenue

Ragtime Vintage Clothing
20 East Walnut Street

Small Terrain
smallterrain.com
278 Haywood Road

Union
unionasheville.com
18 Haywood Street

MARKETS AND FESTIVALS

—

Asheville City Market
(seasonal)
asapconnections.org

The Big Crafty
thebigcrafty.com

Moogfest
moogfest.com

West Asheville Tailgate Market
westashevilletailgatemarket.com
718 Haywood Road

LEISURE

—

Asheville Art Museum
ashevilleart.org
2 South Pack Square

Biltmore Estate
biltmore.com
One Lodge Street

Black Mountain Museum + Arts Center
blackmountaincollege.org
56 Broadway Street

Blue Ridge Parkway
blueridgeparkway.org

Fine Arts Theater
fineartstheatre.com
36 Biltmore Avenue

The Grey Eagle
thegreyeagle.com
185 Clingman Avenue

Penland School of Crafts
penland.org
67 Doras Trail
Penland, North Carolina

Pisgah National Forest
fs.usda.gov/nfsnc

CHARLESTON

RESTAURANTS, CAFÉS, AND BARS

—

Bertha's Kitchen
2332 Meeting Street Road

Bin 152
bin152.com
152 King Street

Black Tap Coffee
blacktapcoffee.com
70½ Beaufain Street

Butcher & Bee
butcherandbee.com
654 King Street

FIG
eatatfig.com
232 Meeting Street

The Ordinary
eattheordinary.com
544 King Street

Royal American
theroyalamerican.com
970 Morrison Drive

Two Boroughs Larder
twoboroughslarder.com
186 Coming Street

Xiao Bao Biscuit
xiaobaobiscuit.com
224 Rutledge Avenue

SHOPS

—

Billy Reid
billyreid.com
150 King Street

Goat Sheep Cow
goatsheepcow.com
106 Church Street

Heirloom Books
heirloombookcompany.com
54½ Broad Street

Indigo & Cotton
indigoandcotton.com
79 Cannon Street

Rogue Wave Surf Shop
roguewavesurfshop.com
69 Spring Street

MARKETS

—

Charleston Farmers' Market
charlestonfarmersmarket.com
Marion Square

LEISURE

—

Charles Towne Landing
friendsofcharlestownelanding.org
1500 Olde Towne Road

Coastal Expeditions
coastalexpeditions.com
514 Mill Street
Mount Pleasant

The Pour House
charlestonpourhouse.com
1977 Maybank Highway

Terrace Theater
terracetheater.com
1956 Maybank Highway

ATHENS

RESTAURANTS AND CAFÉS

—

5 & 10
fiveandten.com
1653 South Lumpkin Street

Farm Cart
farm255.com/farmcart

The Grit
thegrit.com
199 Prince Avenue

Home.made Supper Club
homemade-catering.com
1072 Baxter Street

Ike & Jane Cafe and Bakery
ikeandjane.com
1307 Prince Avenue

The National
thenationalrestaurant.com
232 West Hancock Avenue

Shotgun Dinners
shotgundinners.com

White Tiger
whitetigergourmet.com
217 Hiawassee Avenue

SHOPS

—

Agora
260 West Clayton Street

Avid Bookshop
avidbookshop.com
493 Prince Avenue

Community
119 North Jackson Street

Daily Groceries
dailygroceries.org
523 Prince Avenue

Normal Hardware
1328 Prince Avenue

Treehouse Kid and Craft
treehousekidandcraft.com
815 West Broad Street

MARKETS

—

Athens Farmers' Market
(seasonal)
athensfarmersmarket.net
Bishop Park and Downtown Athens

LEISURE

—

40 Watt Club
40watt.com
285 West Washington Street

**ATHICA: Athens Institute
for Contemporary Art**
athica.org
160 Tracy Street

Ciné
athenscine.com
234 West Hancock Avenue

Georgia Museum of Art
georgiamuseum.org
90 Carlton Street

**Historic North Campus of the
University of Georgia**
Broad Street at College Avenue

Field Trip
(seasonal installations)
ourfieldtrip.com

State Botanical Garden of Georgia
botgarden.uga.edu
2450 South Milledge Avenue

Tree That Owns Itself
*corner of Dearing and
South Finley Streets*

Acknowledgments

·֍◇֍·

Thank you to everyone who supports handmade products and to all the people who dedicate their lives to making them. Thank you to the makers who welcomed me into your spaces for allowing me to photograph you, and for being so open with your time.

A special thanks to Mom, Dad, Brandon, and Noah for your unwavering support and interest.

To Jen Altman: I appreciate all the company, meals, and laughs shared during the making of the book. You are always an inspiration in the way you live your life and in your words and work.

Thank you to Linda Ketelhut and Rinne Allen for sharing ideas and motivation. You are both special talents and inspire me often.

Thank you to everyone at Princeton Architectural Press, especially my editor, Megan Carey, for her endless hours of work, and Elana Schlenker for her beautiful design and vision. And thank you to Becca Barnet for sharing her wonderful illustration talents on the Makers Map.

Also available in this series:
Brooklyn Makers
Jennifer Causey
978-1-61689-074-2

———————— ·❀◇❀· ————————

Published by
Princeton Architectural Press
37 East Seventh Street
New York, New York 10003

Visit our website at papress.com.

Editor: Megan Carey
Designer: Elana Schlenker

Special thanks to: Meredith Baber, Sara Bader,
Nicola Bednarek Brower, Janet Behning, Fannie Bushin,
Carina Cha, Andrea Chlad, Barbara Darko, Benjamin English,
Russell Fernandez, Will Foster, Jan Haux, Emily Johnston-O'Neill,
Diane Levinson, Jennifer Lippert, Katharine Myers, Lauren Palmer,
Margaret Rogalski, Jay Sacher, Rob Shaeffer, Dan Simon,
Sara Stemen, Andrew Stepanian, Paul Wagner, and
Joseph Weston of Princeton Architectural Press
—Kevin C. Lippert, publisher

Library of Congress Cataloging-in-Publication Data
Causey, Jennifer, 1973–
Southern makers : food, design, craft, and other
scenes from the tactile life / Jennifer Causey.
pages cm
ISBN 978-1-61689-164-0 (pbk.)
1. Handicraft—Southern States—Pictorial works.
2. Artisans—Southern States—Interviews.
3. Food—Southern States—Pictorial works.
4. Cooks—Southern States—Interviews.
5. Southern States—Social life and customs. I. Title.
TT23.5.C38 2013
745.50975—dc23
2013014189